T0360882

"Michael Staudacher is a clear-headed businessman who took his extensive life experience and made sense of it in a systematic way. He wrote this up in an accessible, practical, well-organized format. This book has examples, humour, and backbone. It will help non-Germans, from Asia or elsewhere, survive in German business. It is a good read with a clear purpose, and I warmly recommend it."

Prof. Dr. Gert Jan Hofstede
Artificial Sociality, Wageningen University & Research (WUR),
Co-Author of Cultures and Organizations (McGraw-Hill, 2010)

"Very easy to read. Michael Staudacher uses simple day-to-day examples to illustrate the cultural and behavioral differences when dealing with Germans. This is a must-read book for someone who is new to German culture and needs to interact with them regularly, especially a new joiner to a German company."

CS Chua
President and Managing Director,
Infineon Technologies Asia Pacific

To all my colleagues, managers, and partners
who worked with me in the past 30 years.
Especially to the teams in Munich, Regensburg, Taipei,
Bangalore, Corbeil-Essonnes, Portland, Villach, Melaka,
Kulim, and Singapore.
Without you, this book would not have been possible.

PLAYING
BY THE RULES

Understanding German
Business Culture

PLAYING
BY THE RULES
Understanding German Business Culture

Michael Staudacher

World Scientific

NEW JERSEY · LONDON · SINGAPORE · BEIJING · SHANGHAI · HONG KONG · TAIPEI · CHENNAI · TOKYO

Published by

World Scientific Publishing Co. Pte. Ltd.

5 Toh Tuck Link, Singapore 596224

USA office: 27 Warren Street, Suite 401-402, Hackensack, NJ 07601

UK office: 57 Shelton Street, Covent Garden, London WC2H 9HE

Library of Congress Control Number: 2021943216

British Library Cataloguing-in-Publication Data
A catalogue record for this book is available from the British Library.

PLAYING BY THE RULES
Understanding German Business Culture

ISBN 978-981-123-341-8 (hardcover)
ISBN 978-981-123-342-5 (ebook for institutions)
ISBN 978-981-123-343-2 (ebook for individuals)

For any available supplementary material, please visit
https://www.worldscientific.com/worldscibooks/10.1142/12185#t=suppl

Desk Editor: Nicole Ong

Typeset by Stallion Press
Email: enquiries@stallionpress.com

Printed in Singapore

Contents

Introduction

THE IRON LADY

We met for a five-day workshop in Frankfurt. The meeting room was in a private area of our company headquarters, and we had to pass a security guard each time we entered or left the room. We went in and out quite often, leaving for coffee breaks, lunch, picking up guests, and so on. Altogether, I passed the security guard more than 20 times that week. The guard was a nice lady in her mid-40s. I would smile at her and show her my ID card, and she would smile at me and release the gate so that I could pass.

On the last day of the workshop, I brought with me a special gift for a senior member in our team to celebrate his promotion. The gift — a flower in a wooden frame — was quite heavy, so I had to carry it with both hands. As usual, I approached the security lady and smiled at her, but the gate remained closed. So, I smiled even more, but still the gate was closed. Why isn't she opening the gate? I wondered. Finally, I said, "Could you please open the gate?"

"Show me your identity card," she replied in a serious tone.

I had to put the gift on the floor, dig out my ID card, and show it to her once again. Only then did she return my smile and open the gate. What the hell!? I thought. I'd passed the guard more than 20 times — she knew me and my ID card by heart yet she wouldn't open the gate without me showing the card again.

Welcome to rules and regulations, welcome to Germany.

This book gives you insights into the German culture, showing you how to engage with Germans, how to understand what they mean, and how to respond accordingly. I'll share fundamental knowledge that you can use immediately when engaging with Germans, whether in business communication, your private life, or during a holiday. The main objective of this book is to enable you to understand the behavior of your German colleagues, business partners, and/or friends.

I won't go through the German culture from A to Z and touch on every detail. The more points covered, the less information people can recall when they really need it — for example, in a stressful situation. Instead, I focus on the three most important points when engaging with Germans:

- **Directness:** YES means yes and NO means no. Germans say what they mean. Germans place a high value on honesty and this is reflected in their direct way of speaking. What they say is straightforward and candid.
- **Adherence:** You find rules, regulations, and bureaucracy all over the world, but in Germany, they are strictly followed, with no exceptions considered. The case study at the start of this introduction illustrates this strict adherence to rules and regulations. The focus of the guard wasn't on whether a person was authorized to pass the gate or not; her focus was on checking the ID card as per the rule.
- **Commitment:** There is no other culture where commitment is of such importance. Whether it's a promise, a delivery deadline, or just punctuality, Germans stick to their commitments! They know that failing to honor a commitment has an impact on their reputation, meaning that they will be labelled as unreliable.

In today's global businesses, intercultural communication plays a major role. Something as simple as challenging a decision in a meeting or making a vague commitment can lead to misunderstandings that put a project's success at risk. The major challenge is that a misunderstanding isn't always immediately perceived as such. If a misunderstanding leads to open discussion or puts a project on hold, that's fine — the issue is clearly visible and all parties have the same understanding. However, in reality project work can continue but make little progress because team members are at cross purposes. Mergers and acquisitions, international matrix organizations, and global projects all rely on a common understanding; you need to be able to express yourself in a way your counterpart[1] understands, and vice versa.

Chapters 1 and 2 get into the basics of intercultural communication and the German culture, and Chapters 3 to 5 cover in detail three key German habits. Chapter 6 deals with the German understanding of service, and Chapters 7 and 8 cover various business and leisure topics. Chapter 9 re-emphasizes the most important points of the book, and then the appendixes cover frequently asked questions, and facts and figures about Germany.

You may find some statements in this book controversial (especially if you are German). Intercultural communication is mostly based on the intangible and the unconscious, like perceptions and emotions. Some statements in this book are confirmed by statistics, but in general the essence of culture isn't something that can be illustrated by formulas or proven by assured evidence. The information in this book has been gleaned from my 20-plus years visiting, living, and working in multiple countries — from questions asked and feedback given, actions observed, cause and effects seen; to listening to people and understanding what they said and what they meant.

---

[1] I use the term "counterpart" throughout to refer to the "Gegenüber," the person with whom you're interacting, be it your spouse, a colleague, a business partner, your manager, or a foreigner you meet.

Daily life offers up an abundance of information and learnings. Your teacher is the present moment — just observe and learn.

Clarifying Key Terminology

I would like to clarify some of the key terminology used in the following chapters. In this book — and other books about intercultural communication — you often read about:

- Direct and indirect cultures
- Fact-oriented and relationship-oriented cultures
- Face

Direct and indirect cultures

In direct cultures, people tend to communicate in a direct way. Messages are short, truthful, and efficient. They are not wrapped in a context to soften negative content. Sentences are open and frank. People don't beat around the bush, and they expect a quick response to their messages.

In indirect cultures, people can see direct communication as harsh and impolite. Indirect cultures express messages in a polite and soft manner. Part of the message is delivered "between the lines," requiring the recipient to consider the surrounding context. Responses are usually given after a silent "thinking period." A lack of response is interpreted as disagreement.

Fact-oriented and relationship-oriented cultures

In fact-oriented cultures (also called task-oriented cultures), achieving a goal comes before personal relationships. Tasks are thoroughly planned and managed over time. Decision-making is based on facts. Different opinions and conflicts are brought to the table and discussed openly, sometimes in a harsh and offending manner. Success is defined as getting a job done as planned.

In relationship-oriented cultures, people achieve goals through relationships. A person's network is very important. Decisions are made in a group, usually after a broad consensus is reached. Conflicts are handled in small groups or in bilateral talks, to avoid embarrassing confrontations in public. Success is defined by harmony and consensus, and relationships come before plans and schedules.

Direct communication and fact orientation are usually inherent in the same countries; for example, Germany, Russia, and the Netherlands. The same goes for indirect communication and relationship orientation: Both behaviors are common in Japan, India, China, and Saudi Arabia.

Face

The most important matter in a relationship-oriented culture is your face. "Face" in this context means your social standing and reputation in public — how other people perceive you as an individual. For example, do you keep your emotions under control, or do you lose your temper in public? Face is extremely important, especially in Asian cultures. Losing face is seen as embarrassing, a loss of honor, or even shameful. It can damage a personal reputation and impact a person's relationships with other people and groups. People who lose face also lose the respect of others.

Here are examples of how to lose face:

- Insulting individuals in front of others.
- Criticizing people in front of others (this would be a loss of face for the person who criticizes and for the person being criticized).
- Openly disagreeing with elders in countries whereby seniority is highly valued (e.g. Korea and Japan).

- A subordinate pointing out a mistake made by a superior in the organization.
- Being impolite, downplaying peers, and aggressively putting him or herself ahead of the peer group.
- Shouting and showing anger in public.

The challenge is that people from many Western cultures are not familiar with the concept of face at all. They don't care about losing face, and they don't recognize it when they did something that led to someone else losing face. On the contrary, people from Asian cultures will avoid losing face at all costs.

In intercultural communication, face is the topic with the highest potential for disruption. If you caused someone to lose face, it can impact your relationship for years. And the embarrassed person will rarely tell you this. Your relationship will get stuck and you won't know why.

These fundamentally different views on how to communicate and the value of facts and relationships in society are the main source of intercultural misunderstanding. Most of the challenges, characteristics, and solutions discussed in this book are based on the fundamentals of communication, relationships, and — in some cases — face.

About the Author

What qualifies me to talk about the German culture?

I lived in Germany for more than ten years. During this time, I worked for and with German companies and also for a United States multinational company in their German headquarters. I have seen projects succeed and fail. I have many years of experience in doing business with Germans, establishing cooperation between the fact-oriented Germans and people from relationship-oriented cultures, such as Chinese, Indian and Malaysian. I lived in Singapore for a couple of years, and over more than 15 years, I have run projects in Taiwan, China, Malaysia, and India.

I'm a native Austrian; no kangaroos, no Great Barrier Reef — not Australia, but mountains, skiing, and Vienna instead. Austria is a small country adjacent to Germany, with German as its official language. The Austrian culture is quite similar to the German one; most people with a non-European background probably wouldn't notice any difference. But there are differences: Austrian culture has more of a focus on relationships and a higher degree of flexibility in adherence to rules, for example.

I would say that about 60% of my personality is non-German, which means I see most German behaviors curiously; for example, the adherence to rules and regulations, the low level of flexibility, and the lack of spontaneous decisions. For the remaining 40%, I have German traits, especially when it comes to direct communication and the expectation of commitments being honored.

For the most part, the content in this book originates from my personal experience in intercultural communication — situations I encountered or witnessed. Some of the case studies are written from my German view, these are the situations where I describe an interaction with non-German cultures, for example, when I was working with Chinese or Americans. The other case studies are written from my non-German view. These are situations I encountered when engaging with German nationals, for example, the bureaucracy and the strict adherence to regulations.

In all those years of working in an exciting intercultural environment, I learned to identify issues that make all collaborative efforts null and void. For this book, I have chosen to cover the three characteristics with the highest potential to create conflict and misunderstanding: directness, adherence, and commitment.

Chapter 1

Intercultural Communication

Plenty of literature on intercultural communication is available, such as books and reports on studies. An Amazon search for "intercultural" returns more than 20,000 results. Other sources of information are documentaries, movies, and intercultural training courses. The topic pops up in every global company.

What comes to mind when you work with people from other cultures? Do you think:

— *Why do people behave so strangely?* From your perspective, you explained and clarified everything. But the results are totally different from what you expected, and you have no idea why.
— *Why are they still complaining? I did exactly what they asked me to do.* You've done a great job, you've given your best, yet your colleague is complaining about everything. *What's wrong with them?* You wonder.
— *Why are they treating me so badly? Why are they being so offensive? Do they have a problem with me on a personal level?*

Such issues crash any project or cooperation, and they prevent global organizations from being effective. These, and similar situations, are the typical result of intercultural misunderstandings. Learning how people of different cultures communicate gives you valuable insights so that you can minimize misunderstandings.

Objectives of Intercultural Learning

The major objectives of intercultural learning are as follows:

- **Mutual understanding:** As long as you don't understand what your counterpart is trying to express, you can't build a relationship. In order to build mutual understanding, you need to know what someone really wants from you, and that can mean considering more than just the words they say. A message comes with content, feelings, and opinions.[1] You have to consider all sides of a message to know what someone wants and how to react accordingly. It's an advantage of the German communication style that you can mainly focus on the spoken or written word without having to pay much attention to the surrounding context or reading between the lines. The content matters most (Germany has what's called a "low-context culture"[2]).

- **Acceptance:** Once you have clearly understood your counterpart's communication (spoken or written), you are ready to respond; for example, by carrying out their request or agreeing to their proposal. When your counterpart's statement matches your expectations, you can accept it. If not, discuss it until you are mutually happy. The common objective in this phase is to reach a win-win situation.

- **Appreciation:** You've come to a mutual agreement, delivered the desired results, and gotten positive feedback — now's the point where you really appreciate your counterpart. Once you appreciate them, next time you'll find it easier and faster to achieve understanding and acceptance. There is an essential basis for appreciation: Trust. It's difficult to find one word to describe the pillar of success in intercultural communication, but "trust" nails it down. You trust your counterpart and your counterpart

---

[1] The four-sides model, Friedemann Schulz von Thun, German psychologist.
[2] *Beyond Culture*, Edward T. Hall (1976).

trusts you. This is the final state of appreciation and the basis for a perfect relationship in a business or private life.

What are the Benefits of these Intercultural Learnings?

A major benefit is improved decision-making due to having the same perception of things. Expressing yourself in a way your counterpart understands will mean that you can effectively handle complex topics.

Another benefit is a pleasant atmosphere at international workshops and gatherings. You know those meetings where people kept nodding and agreeing but actually nothing is decided or even brought to the table? Acceptance, appreciation, and trust lead to open discussions where people can speak without fear of negative consequences.

And finally, when both parties learn to accept and admit their failures, an open feedback culture is established — finger-pointings and justifications vanish.

The financial controller is asking, "How much money will this save?" Benefits of soft-skills improvement are quite difficult to measure. In the case of intercultural learning, the obvious benefits to consider are reduced meeting times and, more importantly, faster decisions. So, when you have to argue with your boss to arrange an intercultural training session, or to buy more copies of this great book, highlight these two key benefits: Reduced meeting times and faster decisions.

One final point to remember: You cannot build mutual appreciation and trust just by reading a book or attending an intercultural training session. This is a process that takes months or even years of working closely with your intercultural partners, learning by doing and learning by making failures. In this book, I am just getting you started on some of the most important points to pay attention to when engaging with Germans. Eventually, you will build mutual appreciation and trust.

Getting a Feel of the Culture

"Off the beaten path" is an overused phrase. The places listed in a travel guide under that heading are anything but undiscovered. You find so many "secret and unknown" tips about locations that these places are as touristy as the top landmarks are. To get a good feel of the culture, you should explore on your own.

Whenever you visit a new country, I suggest that you don't just spend your time at the typical tourist spots. Leave your comfort zone and explore — then you'll get to know the real vibe of another culture.

It sounds more complex than it actually is. In many cases, the "off the beaten track" stuff is no more than 1 or 2 kilometers away. Just leave the crowds behind and walk away from the usual landmarks, or use public transport to move farther out. For example, in Munich the typical tourist shopping spots are at the very center — Marienplatz, Kaufingstrasse, and Sendlingerstrasse — fine places to find interesting stuff, no doubt. But instead, jump on an S-Bahn and take a ride of no more than 30 minutes to Neuperlach (PEP shopping center), Duelferstrasse (Mira shopping center), or Olympia-Einkaufszentrum (OEZ shopping center). These are shopping areas with a low number of tourists that give you a better picture of "doing as the locals do."

Individuals versus Culture

Intercultural learning covers a culture, exploring habits, behaviors, and standards. It also offers examples for dealing with individuals, particular situations, or events. Overall, this book describes behaviors *most* people have or things *most* people do; it describes cultural

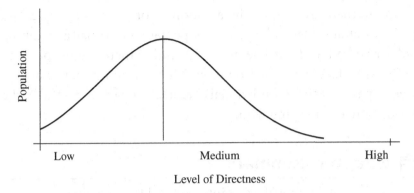

Figure 1: Directness curve (India)

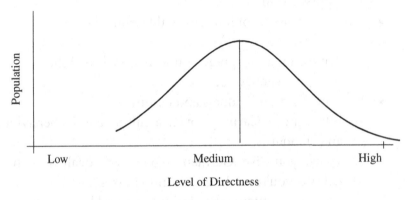

Figure 2: Directness curve (Germany)

standards. For instance, if you outline the population of a country on the Y-axis and how directly people of this country communicate on the X-axis, the chart for India will look like Figure 1, and for Germany, it will look like Figure 2.

Keep in mind: When you visit Germany, you're not dealing with a culture, you're dealing with individuals. The custom officer at the airport, the taxi driver, the hotel receptionist, your colleagues — all these are individual people with individual characters. So, in

Germany, there are people who are indirect or reserved; people who don't care about rules and regulations; people who are bad at planning and arrive half an hour late; just as in India, there are people who are "in your face" with their opinion. With this in mind, you always need to pay attention to individual character, and be respectful to the person you are engaging with.

Chapter Summary

- The main objectives of intercultural learning are:
  - Mutual understanding
  - Acceptance
  - Appreciation
- The main benefits of intercultural learning are:
  - Faster decision-making
  - A pleasant atmosphere at international workshops
  - An open feedback culture
- Keep in mind: Individuals and culture
  - Intercultural learning covers a culture and its behaviors and standards.
  - When you visit Germany, you're not dealing with a culture, you're dealing with individuals.
  - Always pay attention to individuals and be respectful to the person you are communicating with.

Chapter 2

The Germans

Before I cover the three most important characteristics of Germans, in this chapter I start with some basics about the German culture — and I don't mean beer and sausages. Sure, Germans like to drink beer and eat the famous Weisswurst sausage for breakfast, but you can find out about that in any tourist guidebook. If you compete with Germans in drinking beer, you won't need intercultural training at all. During a drinking session, you'll understand each other quite well (at least at the beginning; after a few rounds of beer, listening and especially talking get increasingly difficult...).

This chapter gives you insights into how Germans behave and why. You need to know the core values of Germans to understand their decision-making processes.

Unlike most of the Asian cultures, Germans have a fact-oriented culture (see "Clarifying key terminology" in the Introduction). Countries like Malaysia, China, India, and Singapore are relationship-oriented. Fact-oriented cultures have different core values than relationship-oriented cultures. These are the core values of German culture:

- Candor
- Reliability
- Commitment
- Respect for facts and figures

You don't need a personal relationship to do business with Germans. Offering a service or a product that is better or cheaper than a competitor's puts you in their favor. It doesn't matter whether you are new in the market or already have a long-term record. It doesn't matter whether you paint the town red every night or are devoted to your family. Germans rarely consider personal background when making a business decision.

In business discussions, the decision-making processes are based on facts — for example, the features of your product; the quality and scope of your service; or the outcome of analysis, statistics, or surveys. Objective facts come first, and interpersonal relations play a secondary role. As an example, consider someone buying a new TV set. In Asia, the person will ask a friend who may know something about TVs, someone in their personal network who has experience and can recommend a specific brand or model. In Germany, the person will buy a professional TV journal or a magazine specializing in consumer tests. They'd choose the TV based on test results or recommendations by experts. Magazines featuring consumer tests are very popular. Basically, they test everything — all kinds of electronic goods, vacuum cleaners, light bulbs; vegetables, bread, sausages, water; even doormats, toilet paper, and pregnancy tests. The opinions of subject-matter experts are highly valued in Germany, higher than a recommendation from a friend or someone in their personal network.

The core values of relationship-oriented cultures are face, relationships, and harmony. These core values are the opposite to the core values of fact-oriented cultures. For example, if you are honest and admit to your failures in public, this will be appreciated and treated as candor in Germany, but you will lose face in most Asian countries.

Values are inherited over generations. They are learned during childhood, developed in the teenage years, and strengthened in the day-to-day life throughout adulthood. Values influence the behavior of people on a large scale. In communication and in attitude, each reply and behavior is driven by a subconscious core value.

Further German core values are expertise, quality, work-life balance, and privacy. Other values of relationship-oriented cultures are education, religion, and respect for elders. There is no real overlap; only some values are shared by both cultures — family — to name one. But even with family, differences exist. In Germany, "family" covers the children, the partner, and probably the parents. In India, every sister, brother, uncle, and far-off relative belongs to the family. So, in general, there is a big gap between the Germans and relationship-oriented cultures. It's an objective of intercultural learning to overcome this gap.

As mentioned in Chapter 1, you cannot reach mutual appreciation and trust just by reading a book or by attending an intercultural training course. The same applies to core values. You can't change core values in a month or two, if you can change them at all (I discourage you from trying to change core values). But you can become aware of the values, so that you understand your counterpart's behavior and more importantly, you understand your own behavior and its roots: Your core values.

Quality

Germans take quality very seriously. It's most probably the value for which Germans are best known by the rest of the world. A German product is considered reliable; quality control in manufacturing is a top priority. Sometimes, you find this need for quality in people's behavior. Germans tend to be perfectionists. Everything must be at the highest standard; only products with zero flaws are released. This is a great trait for specific industries — like the automotive, medical, and transport industries — and in these industries, German companies have leading positions: BMW, Audi, Mercedes, Bayer, Siemens, and others. However, perfectionism can be a stumbling block in other industries where time-to-market and flexibility are key, like consumer electronics, mobile devices, and gaming. In these industries, United States (US), Korean, and Chinese companies are ruling the market.

Private Life and Privacy

This book often mentions the separation of private life and business life. In relationship-oriented cultures, regular business dinners with your department, your managers, or business partners are part of standard business conduct. Germans prefer to meet family or friends after work or just stay at home. Private circles of friends are kept separate from colleagues and business acquaintances, and socializing with colleagues isn't as common as in other cultures. Business events are rare: Maybe a team event once a quarter where the whole team goes out for dinner, or a celebration event like the annual Christmas party.

However, it's interesting to note that once the team does come together, the event may continue until quite late. I remember attending many business dinners in India, Taiwan, and Malaysia. Most of them took about three to four hours and finished before ten or eleven p.m. A celebration event in Germany often goes on until midnight or later. I've been to events where I left at midnight and one third of the people were still celebrating. Some regulars will make it until four a.m. (don't expect them to be in the office next morning, though!).

When you visit colleagues in Germany, don't expect them to take you out for dinner or show you around every night. They may go out with you once or twice a week, but for the remaining time, they'll leave you alone because they respect your private life and want to give you time for yourself. They believe that showing you around all the time is an intrusion into your privacy. And privacy is highly protected: Germany has one of the strictest privacy laws in the world.

Global companies like Facebook,[1] Google,[2] and Microsoft[3] have data protection and privacy issues in Germany. When Google Street View enabled the blurring of private houses, they remarked that the public opposition to Street View in Germany had been tougher than in any other country: More than 240,000 households have opted out of Street View.[4]

Moaning and Complaining

Another German behavior is focusing on the negative: The glass is half-empty, so to say. It's not that Germans only bring up negative things, it's just that when they respond to a question, the first thing they may mention is something bad or something that's not working. You'll notice this with individuals you meet in town, and colleagues or business partners you work with.

Even the media communicates in this way. Glancing at German newspaper headlines will make you think the end of the world is nigh! A hot summer means global warming, a bad day at the stock market will lead to the next economic crisis, North Korea launches a test rocket and World War III is imminent, and so on. Another good example is when the Euro depreciated against other currencies. The nationwide newspapers declared

---

[1] The Verge, "Germany orders Facebook to stop collecting data on WhatsApp users," http://www.theverge.com/2016/9/27/13071330/facebook-whatsapp-user-data-germany-privacy.

[2] PC World, "Google ordered by German authority to change privacy practices," http://www.pcworld.com/article/2907612/google-ordered-by-german-authority-to-change-privacy-practices.html.

[3] CNN Tech, "Microsoft to store data in Germany to keep it from third parties," http://money.cnn.com/2015/11/11/technology/microsoft-germany-data-center-privacy.

[4] DW.com, "More than 244,000 opt out of Google Street View in Germany," http://www.dw.com/en/more-than-244000-opt-out-of-google-street-view-in-germany/a-6133854.

that "that's the end of the European Union," instead of focusing on the great opportunities that a lower currency could give the local export-oriented companies. The positive side of a story is usually mentioned later, or not at all. The media's motto is "no news is good news," and you can assume that things not mentioned in the news are running well.

Germans love moaning and complaining. I noticed this most of all when I was working for a multinational corporation in Munich. We had quite a big canteen with shared tables. When I was at lunch, I couldn't help but listen to the conversations of others at the table. The majority involved complaining about colleagues or certain circumstances:

- "Oh, Andreas didn't deliver the report on time."
- "I've told her this plenty of times, and she still doesn't understand."
- "I've done my tasks, but the purchasing team didn't deliver on time, so we couldn't finish this project."

The common theme throughout the moaning spree was people blaming others — but not themselves — it was always someone else's fault. This mindset is self-focused and one-sided. Putting the blame on others implies that you did everything right: "I was perfect... and the failing was Team's XYZ's fault." But this judgement completely misses the big picture and blocks out-of-the-box thinking like "What could I have done better?"

A blaming mindset causes particular trouble in projects. A person or a team delivers on time but doesn't care what other teams are doing. Working in project teams requires a broad focus, seeing the big picture independent from one's own deliveries. It's great when someone delivers perfectly on time, but it doesn't help to achieve the project goal if other teams don't deliver on the same level.

It seems to be the case that Germans are happy when they are subordinates and must do what they're told, and do so perfectly. It's rare that outstanding people emerge from this crowd, but thankfully, they have done so more and more in recent years, especially in senior management positions.

Coming from another culture — especially from the US, where there is a strong focus on the positive — it can be difficult to get used to this moaning. Americans may take offense to Germans complaining, thinking that their work is being put in a bad light because Germans are highlighting what's not working and blaming everyone else but themselves. I experienced this when the German company I worked for was bought by an American multinational corporation with a strong and direct US-driven culture. Our office was located in Germany with mainly German employees and senior leaders. Gradually, more and more US leaders were integrated into the German organization, yet it still took years for the mindset of the whole organization to change from a moaning German style to a cheering US style. OK, that's a bit of an exaggeration: We met in the middle somehow, which was a great mixture of the best of both cultures. We focused on the overall goal, made sure that the teams thought outside of the box, and openly discussed things that were not working. However, keep in mind that this progress took years. Patience is key.

Working with Germans means rerouting their energy from focusing on the bad to focusing on the overall objective, the big picture.

Perception of the Culture

I've visited Thailand quite often over the years. If you move away from the typical tourist places, you find the real Thailand and its terrific people (see "Getting a feel of a culture" in Chapter 1).

Wherever you go — to a shop, a restaurant, a street-food stall, a hidden temple — you feel welcomed and are greeted with a smile. People move at a slow and calm pace. There is a reason Thailand's nickname is the 'Land of Smiles.'

You find a similar atmosphere in other Asian cities too. In Ho Chi Minh City, Vietnam, thousands of motorbikes crisscross through the streets, apparently without any rules, and the air is filled with the sound of honking horns. Western media often publishes photos of such scenes, and when you look at these images, the whole situation seems like absolute chaos. But when you visit Ho Chi Minh City yourself, you see that amidst all this hustle, there is serenity. This serenity isn't in the environment, it's in the people. You see it in their eyes, their expressions, their body language, and their tone of voice; their small reactions and movements. Honking, chaos — yet, a calm place. How come?

These subtle messages, unconsciously sent to the outside environment and unconsciously perceived by others, are called micro-messages.[5] Micro-messages may be 'micro', but they affect how you feel when you're in unfamiliar surroundings. Micro-messaging exists in every culture and these messages are sent by every individual. The subject of micro-messaging doesn't have the level of public attention it deserves, but lately, it has been added to the standard training catalog of multinational companies. I see micro-messaging as a major factor in how people are perceived by others.

Let's look at Germans now. Germans move quickly and assertively. They have a clear destination in mind and move precisely towards it. They see anything that gets in their way as disruptive. Their facial expressions can be tense, their gaze focused and piercing, their tone of voice anxious.

---

[5] Stephen Young, *Micromessaging: Why Great Leadership Is Beyond Words* (McGraw-Hill Education, 2006).

Here are the micro-messages relating to Germans and the potential unconscious interpretations:

Perception: What you see	Unconscious interpretation: You think people are...
People are busy worrying. There's the sense that something must be done or they won't achieve their goal. There's an undercurrent of fear.	Anxious
They can't sit still; they keep moving, looking for something (for what?)	Restless
People are moving fast, hurrying. There's no time for small talk. They seem to be thinking, *Get out of my way.*	Stressed
People sigh often and aren't happy with their current situation; they must change the situation. They question everything (except the rules and regulations.)	Frustrated
They have a sad facial expression, like something's gone wrong. *Leave me alone. I don't want to talk.*	Sad
Their gazes are piercing. They don't like me, or have an issue with someone.	Hatred
They complain in an anxious tone. *All is wrong, all is bad. It's all someone else's fault.*	Negative
People ignore me completely; they don't say hello. They keep conversation to the bare minimum, speaking in short sentences.	Distant, reserved, arrogant

Unconsciously, we sum up the micro-messages that we receive and form a perception of a country and its population based on the most dominant messages. For Asian countries like Thailand or Vietnam, this perception might be happiness or serenity; for Germany, it's more likely anxiety and negativity.

Arrogance is a strong perception. People in Germany are short-spoken, and in some situations, you can feel completely ignored. Even in neighboring German-speaking countries like Austria and Switzerland, Germans are perceived as arrogant. However, the perception of arrogance is also driven by the language dialect. Germans speak "standard German" (also called High German), which is basically German without any dialect and it sounds intellectual. It's a bit similar to American and British English. A British farmer speaking perfect Oxford English might sound arrogant to a Texan cowboy without actually being arrogant.

It's important to understand that perceptions and reality can be different. Keep in mind that people are individuals (see "Individuals versus culture" in Chapter 1). Say someone is late for an appointment: That person may be having family trouble, broken off a relationship, or is simply having a cold. All these events lead to similar micro-messages. Be careful: Don't stereotype and lump everyone together.

The roots of these cultural micro-messages aren't entirely clear. Why do Germans behave as they do? Is it because of the painful history of Germany — the World Wars, the sufferings incurred by Germans, and the sufferings Germans caused? I doubt this theory. Vietnam has a similar sad history and people there don't exude sadness or frustration. Some people say that it was because Germans are so used to following rules that a leader like Hitler could cause the country's population to act as they did in World War II. Who knows? And this still wouldn't explain why they follow rules; what is the root cause?

Anyway, I don't want to write an essay on German sociology here, and I don't want to judge: Nothing is good or bad, it is just different. The German economy is one of the strongest in the world, hence their behaviors cannot be only bad.

Ultimately, you need to avoid getting overwhelmed by the negativity in the air. And take care if you live in Germany for a long time: Negativity is contagious.

Chapter Summary

- German core values are:
  - Candor
  - Reliability
  - Commitment
  - Respect for facts and figures
  - Expertise
  - Quality
  - Family
  - Recreation
  - Privacy
- In business discussions, the decision-making processes are based on facts.
- Business and private lives are separated.
- Privacy and data protection are highly valued and are controlled by law.
- Don't expect to be taken for dinner or shown around every night.
- Germans love moaning and complaining, especially about others.
- Don't get overwhelmed by the negativity in the air. It's part of the culture and not meant to be offensive.

Chapter 3

Key Characteristic #1 — Directness

Directness is the most obvious characteristic which strikes you when communicating with Germans. Yes means yes, and no means no!

When asking questions like "What do you think about my solution?" and "Do you agree with my proposal?", don't be surprised when you get answers like "This doesn't work!", "No, I don't agree," and "That's impossible." In a situation where you ask for help, your counterpart may simply respond, "No, I'm sorry, but currently I have no time."

It's important to understand that such answers aren't meant to offend — Germans just say what they mean. They can make the situation quite clear with just one word, "Yes" or "No," and they don't hesitate to put across their views in this direct way. There's no reading between the lines, analyzing the context, or gauging subtext from body language and facial expressions. Germans just listen to what you say and concentrate on facts and figures. They don't beat around the bush, but communicate directly and clearly.

In relationship-oriented cultures, small talk plays an important part in communication. Before you get down to the nitty-gritty, you cover topics such as matters of current interest, the journey, hotel, food, and hobbies. Small talk is "big talk" in many cases. It gives you the chance to find out things about the background of the other person. Before talking about facts, you try to get a picture of who the person is.

In Germany, small talk is more or less non-existent. At the first meeting, topics like the weather or your journey to Germany are touched upon with a few sentences. But that's it; immediately after this, you get down to business. In subsequent meetings, Germans usually skip small talk and discuss business matters directly.

JUST A WASTE OF TIME

In 2014, a German company launched a project to improve the logistics process in Malaysia. The purpose of the project was to introduce a new delivery process that would reduce cost and freight in the company's logistic hub in Penang. The project manager was Chinese and the majority of the team members were Germans.

To align the project status on a regular basis, the project manager scheduled a weekly conference call. The first question of the call was always, "How are you?" Next, the project manager would talk about the weather, the meal he'd had the previous evening, German football teams, and further topics that had nothing to do with the project. After a few minutes, he would start to discuss project-related items. It was the same procedure every week: About ten minutes of small talk before he got down to business.

The German team members were quite confused by this small talk, and soon most of them would join the call a few minutes after schedule, to avoid wasting time. For the Chinese project manager, the small talk was very important — to build his relationship with the team. For the German colleagues, though, it was just a waste of time. The Chinese project manager felt offended when the German team members joined the call 10 to 15 minutes late. The project became stuck, because trust was not established and nobody spoke out openly about what was bothering them.

Small talk is fine when you meet a German for the first time or you haven't spoken for a few weeks. But skip small talk when you communicate with someone on a regular basis. Get down to business directly.

When you attend an intercultural training course to help you work with Germans, you will learn that you can say the word "No" easily and directly. But don't be surprised if, when you do, an immediate "Why not?" comes back. If you reject or refuse something, be prepared to have fact-based arguments ready to explain why. Also don't hesitate to demand details if your German colleague gives you a "no." Ask, "What's the basis for your opinion?", or "Can you please explain your statement in detail?", or simply "Why not?"

Sometimes, the German communication style can seem confrontational. When they address a problem or an issue, they come straight to the point. There's no paraphrasing of the issue, no attempt to prevent the person-in-charge from losing face. They highlight problems directly; they even express criticism of the person-in-charge openly.

When Germans address an issue in your area of responsibility, don't take it as personal disapproval. They're just explaining — in a direct manner — the issue by stating objective facts. They express bluntly what went wrong, without mentioning what went well, and without considering whether they may be causing offense. Their priority is to fix the issue as soon as possible, not to hurt or to blame someone.

The same goes with conflict. If there's a conflict between two people, it needs to be solved. During my cooperation with Chinese colleagues, I noticed people or workgroups having completely different views and subsequent conflicts remaining unresolved for a long time. But still, these people worked together in perfect harmony as if no conflicts or disputes existed. Amazing! In Germany that's not possible. If there's a conflict between two people, it needs to be resolved as soon as possible. Therefore, Germans address a conflict directly, sometimes even in public. Resolving a conflict can end up in a loud discussion that includes insults. However, this direct approach usually resolves conflicts quite quickly. For example, Germans identify a conflict in the morning, resolve it with an emotional discussion in the afternoon, and finally, the parties involved go out for a couple of beers in the evening. By the next day, the conflict is not an obstruction anymore; all that remains is an aching head if they had one over the eight the night before.

In Germany, questions are taken literally. The common English questions "How's it going?" or "How are you doing?" simply mean "Hi" or "Hello." But Germans treat this kind of greeting as "How are you?" and so they will tell you how they're feeling or doing. And sometimes, this can be quite a detailed answer. So, when you ask a question, expect an answer in any case.

Communication is bidirectional: It consists of sending and receiving. We have covered the part on sending: Germans are direct communicators. But the part on receiving is also very important. Issues come up when Germans receive messages from cultures which communicate indirectly. Germans expect their counterpart to communicate directly and clearly; they aren't used to reading between the lines or taking the social context into account. If these expectations aren't understood, it can lead to misunderstandings.

THE NEVER-ENDING STORY

A few years ago, I was leading a project to introduce a new manufacturing software in a Chinese company. The project went well up to a small change of scope. Due to an unplanned event, a few functionalities weren't delivered as promised. But one of these functionalities, the printing option, was committed to the key business user at the start of the project. So, I requested that Hui Wen, the local project contact at the Chinese company, inform Aaron about the scope reduction. Aaron was the local key business user and the spokesperson of the business association.

"Hello, Hui Wen," I said. "Could you please inform Aaron about the missing print functionality?"

"Yes, sure, I will do so," Hui Wen replied. "But can you please clarify the new timeline first?" she added.

(Continued)

(Continued)

> For the following two days, I reworked the project plan and worked out a new schedule for the missing print option.
>
> During my next meeting with Hui Wen, I said, "The users will get the print functionality two months after the end of the project. Could you please inform Aaron now?"
>
> "OK," Hui Wen replied, "but Aaron might be interested in the funding background. Don't you think we should present these budget items, too?"
>
> So, I had to rework my documents again and prepare a presentation regarding the project funding.
>
> The week after, I presented the results to Hui Wen. "So, the new timeline and funding are defined. I've put it all together in a presentation. Could you please check this and present it to the business users?"
>
> "Yes, I will present this at the user meeting," she agreed. "But... I can't attend this week's meeting. I need to finish some backlog first. So, I'll prepare this for next week's meeting."
>
> And of course, next week another reason prevented Hui Wen from presenting. And so, the story goes on and on in this way. Whenever a new reason popped up, I fixed it, and then something else happened to prevent Aaron from getting the information about the project scope reduction.

What happened in this situation? Why was Hui Wen acting this way? This story has two perspectives — my German view of the situation and Hui Wen's Chinese view. Let's compare them.

First, what did Hui Wen see?

1. Her relationship to Aaron
2. The promise given at the start of the project
3. Her commitment
4. Her reputation

And what did I see?

1. The timeline
2. The funding
3. Hui Wen's availability
4. Business as usual

Now let's analyze the dialogue:

Hui Wen said: "Yes, sure, I will do so. But can you please clarify the new timeline first?"

She really meant: *"We promised Aaron at the beginning. We can't reduce the scope. I can't tell him; I will lose face."*

Next, she said: "OK, but Aaron might be interested in the funding background. Don't you think we should present these budget items, too?"

She really meant: *"I can't tell Aaron. I will lose face."*

And finally, she said: "Yes, I will present this at the user meeting. But I can't attend this week's meeting. I need to finish some backlog first. So, I'll prepare this for next week's meeting."

Which really means: *"Once again, I won't tell Aaron. I will lose face."*

Hui Wen made it quite clear three times that she couldn't tell Aaron without losing face. But what did I understand from her communication?

"Oh, Aaron needs the timeline. OK, I'll provide it."

"Oh, Aaron needs the funding. OK, I'll provide it."

"You aren't available? OK, so next week, you'll present this at the meeting. Fine."

What is the lesson to learn from this story? Don't expect that your German counterpart understands unsaid things. Communicate directly and clearly.

How did the story continue?

> After a while, Hui Wen capitulated and said, "Michael, I can't tell Aaron. I will lose face."

That hit home! Until Hui Wen's clear and open statement, I had no clue what was really going on. At this time, when Hui Wen spoke openly and directly to me, I was really ashamed that I had not recognized her request to find another way to solve the problem. Now, when I look back years after this incident, I see that it gave me one of the most important lessons in my life. This candid talk opened my eyes and inspired in me an enthusiasm for intercultural communication. Without that talk, I never would have written this book.

Extending an Invitation, or Being Invited

The rule is easy: First answer applies! Don't ask your German colleague to dinner at your home just to be polite. Your colleague will take your offer seriously, and the answer will be most likely be, "Yes." You won't have to ask multiple times; you will get the "yes" on your first attempt.

If a German invited you, and you want to accept the invitation, say "yes" the first time, too. Don't expect to be asked multiple times; to say "no" three times and then accept when asked a fourth time. Such invitations are issued just once, so make your first answer the right one.

And by the way, Germans strictly separate their private life from their business life, so it's an honor to be invited by a German to their home.

Giving Feedback

As you may suppose, feedback from Germans is direct and they mean what they say. Especially when discussing results in global business projects, this can be challenging.

KNOW-HOW TRANSFERS GONE WRONG

During a knowledge transfer project, we had training classes where German experts trained engineers from an Indian outsourcing partner. After finishing a couple of these classes, we conducted certification sessions. In these sessions, the Indian outsourcing partner presented their understanding of the training and the German experts would ask them technical questions.

In one of these sessions, a young German engineer asked the Indian team leader a detailed technical question, to verify the team's knowledge. The Indian team had a discussion. A few minutes later, the team leader responded with his answer. As the project was just at its beginning, the answer was incorrect. Immediately, the German engineer responded, "Your answer is totally, totally wrong!", and without hesitating for a second, he explained to them the proper way to solve the problem. The Indian team was astonished. A junior software engineer had embarrassed the experienced and knowledgeable team leader in front of his whole team!

What do you think — why did the German engineer react in such a way? Did he have a personal problem with the Indian team leader? Or did he intend to crash the project?

No, he just wanted to help. He wanted to help the Indian team get the right understanding and find the most effective way to solve the problem (mission accomplished: The Indian team would never forget how to solve this problem and would also never forget this session). Of course, for the Indian team this hit hard, especially for the team leader, who lost face in front of his team. But the German engineer didn't see this; he didn't see the context of the team relations. From the perspective of a relationship-oriented culture, his answer seems offensive. But the German engineer just saw the solution to the problem and wanted to help the Indian partner be more effective in the future. Don't take such feedback personally.

Germans give positive feedback, of course. Here are some examples:

- "In general, OK."
- "It's good."
- "Works as expected."
- "Not bad."

Yes, you read correctly; "Not bad" is a positive feedback in Germany. Adjectives like *outstanding*, *unbelievable*, and *excellent* are used very rarely. If Germans use such words, you can be sure they mean what they say and you really did an outstanding job!

Germans state negative feedback clearly. Some examples are:

- "… must be improved."
- "… is not satisfactory."
- "… was a waste of time."

But don't consider negative feedback to be personal disapproval. Germans offer such feedback to help, to bring the other partner forward, even if they unwittingly offend.

A final point regarding feedback is that in Germany giving *no* feedback means good feedback; it means everything is running fine. Germans tend to see things running well as normal; therefore, often they give no feedback at all. But if something is wrong, they will let you know for sure. Be careful: They expect the same from your side. As long you don't mention issues directly, your German counterpart assumes everything is running as expected.

Losing Face

A word regarding face: The essence of keeping or losing face (see "Face" in the Introduction) — one of the most important matter in Asian cultures — doesn't exist in Germany. If a German refuses to do something or admits that they can't solve a problem, the person won't lose face at all. People might think, *He refuses everything*, or, *This guy is shouting and scolding all the time*, and that leads to a reputation as a denier or even a choleric person. But fact-oriented expertise is still appreciated, independently from personal relations. And if the person changes their behavior, their reputation will change accordingly over time. Don't worry about losing face in Germany.

Chapter Summary

- Don't treat short and direct answers as offensive or disrespectful.
- Express yourself directly, and don't expect Germans to read between the lines.
- If something is unclear, ask immediately and directly for clarification.
- Keep small talk to a minimum.
- No feedback is good feedback.
- Don't treat negative feedback as personal disapproval.
- You won't lose face if you refuse to do something or admit to failing.

Chapter 4

Key Characteristic #2 — Adherence

Bureaucracy, follow the rules, obey the law. Bureaucracy is everywhere in the world, but usually you know someone who can help you get things done. Someone who knows how to bypass regulations, or let's say treat a regulation more "flexibly" (some would say infringe). In Germany, things are different: Regulation is regulation.

Remember my story about the security lady in the Introduction? I passed by the security gate more than 20 times. The lady knew me very well, but she would not let me pass through the gate unless I showed her my identity card. She strictly adhered to a rule without making a single exception. I think even if her mother wanted to go through the gate, she would have to show her ID card.

This strict following of regulations has advantages and disadvantages. A major drawback is that the process runs as it's defined without any exception. There is no possibility to speed it up; you have to go through the full process. In addition, even though the process is documented in meticulous detail, it's conducted by individuals, by humans, and they have their own view on things and their own working style, and they make their own interpretations. This makes German bureaucracy even more difficult to handle. For example, when you call a service hotline three times, you deal with three different people and get three different answers...

On the other hand, there is the advantage that everyone is treated the same, no matter whether they are a managing director, a waitress, or a police officer. Connections (referred to as *"guanxi"* in Chinese) and personal networks don't help a lot. So, the overall duration and the outcome of a bureaucratic process are quite predictable.

In general, rules and regulations are taken very seriously in Germany, especially in German companies. There is a rule or a defined process for nearly everything. If you want to simplify an existing process — to make it less complicated — you can be sure that some colleagues will complain that any step of the process is a must and cannot be eliminated. Even if the elimination of the step will make their life easier, they won't support its removal, because they feel uncertain about changing the process. They see a risk in the removal because it could impact the outcome or product the process was designed for. And it's not just the removal of the step that make Germans feel uncomfortable, it's also the matter of the change itself. Germans don't like change.

Germans' strict adherence to rules sets them apart from other European countries. Italy, Austria, and France have quite similar regulations, but they know when to break them or be flexible.

WHY DO IT EASY IF YOU CAN MAKE IT COMPLICATED

Tom was working for an electronics company headquartered in Germany with manufacturing facilities all over the world. At the beginning of his career, he had been employed by an Austrian facility, and later, he'd moved to a German facility. Both facilities produced the same products and had the same clearly defined processes. But the interpretation was quite different.

When Tom was working in Austria, he needed to order a small memory extension for his computer. He called Marc, the technician responsible for upgrades. Tom succinctly explained his requirements, and the next day, Marc installed the upgrade on Tom's computer. Problem solved.

(*Continued*)

(Continued)

In Germany, to do the same thing Tom needed to fill in an up-grade request form, get the approval from his legal manager, and then send the request to the upgrade advisory board for their approval. Once both parties approved, he raised a purchase order, which had to be approved by the controlling department and the cost center responsible. Finally, the upgrade was ordered. And "only" four weeks later, a technician came around to upgrade the computer. A task that took one day and a phone call in Austria, took six weeks and four approvals in Germany.

Beside the rules in business, many rules also apply in Germans' social life: Do this, do that. For example:

- An official "no noise" resting period from noon to two p.m. in private housing areas.
- No barbequing in your garden without the approval of your neighbor.
- Strict rules in urban parks.
- One-way bicycle lanes.
- Smoking areas in train stations, with yellow lines on the ground designating the area.

Bureaucracy, rules, and regulations are present in many countries. But the major difference in Germany is that people strictly follow the rules. And furthermore, if you don't follow the rules, someone will "remind" or "advise" you to follow them, and this person may not be a policeman. It might be your neighbor or just a pedestrian on the street. If you consistently break regulations — even minor regulations; for example, driving down a private road with your car — other people may note your license plate and report you to a police station. A saying about the Germans goes as follows: "There is a policeman in every German."

THIS IS MY WASTE BIN

I went to a coffee shop in Munich, ordered my non-fat, decaf cappuccino to go, and then strolled around a public park. Eventually, I passed a small sales booth. I took a look at the items, finished my cappuccino, and trashed the cup in the waste bin. As I moved along, suddenly the vendor started to complain. "Hey, this is our waste bin. If you buy something from the coffee shop, use their waste bin." I was so astonished that I couldn't say a word. Anyway, even if I could say something, how should I have responded? So, quite puzzled, I moved along, leaving a head-shaking vendor behind.

In this case, the vendor defined the rule: Only his customers may use his waste bin. Don't be surprised when you encounter all kinds of unwritten rules in all areas of daily life in Germany, and additionally, being notified quickly when you break them.

What are the benefits of all these rules and regulations? First, a clearly defined process. You don't have to think about doing something this way or that way. Most of the tasks are clearly defined and documented. Just follow the process. Second, you can be quite sure that the majority of people will follow the processes as defined. So, when working with Germans, either with government or a German company, you will come across well-defined standard activities that are predictable to perform. If a process description says a process takes two to three weeks, it usually does.

The drawback of the process adherence is loss of flexibility; for example, if a process doesn't run as desired, or no standard process is defined for the task at hand. Germans are not risk-takers — they try to avoid deviations and reduce risks as far as possible. When approaching non-standard procedures, don't expect creativity, flexibility, or spontaneous decisions. Usually, you will face long-lasting discussions with all involved parties before the problem is really tackled.

Because I'm Right

This strict adherence to given rules creates plenty of potential for conflict in daily life. When Germans think they are right (and they probably are), they will do everything to defend and protect their position, even if it makes no sense at all. In many cases, it would take less effort to work around or give up the position, but just because they are right, they will insist on their standpoint. "I'm right" is considered a very inner personal space; and if you intrude upon a person's personal space, they will feel deeply affronted and uncomfortable.

A WRONG TURN

Germany has a great network for cyclists. Even in crowded city centers, roads have a separate lane for bicycles. The principle of separate bicycle lanes is also implemented at pedestrian crossings: The left part of the crossing is reserved for bikes, and the right is for pedestrians. As there are more pedestrians than cyclists, the bicycle lane is smaller, maybe about 1.2 meters (4 feet) wide compared to 3 meters (10 feet) for pedestrians. Both lines are separated by just a marking on the ground. Locals know which side is for bikes and which is for pedestrians. However, if you're new to Germany, this arrangement may not be immediately clear.

Strolling around the city, I encountered such a crossing. Brave as I am, I moved to the very left of the crossing (in the bicycle lane) to give the cyclist as much space as possible. There was just one cyclist, a lady, and no other pedestrians but me. If you were the cyclist, what would you do in this situation, faced with a pedestrian in your bike lane? Well, you'd just use the pedestrian lane to ride around the person in the bike lane and continue. No issue at all, right?

Not so in Germany. The lady continued on her path until she nearly hit me and had to stop her bike. Of course, she read me the riot act, complaining bitterly that I was using the wrong lane. Yes, I confess,

---

(*Continued*)

I was wrong; but why stop the bike and spend a couple of minutes berating me? It wasn't just a complete waste of time for her; she also put herself in a bad emotional state. I looked at her — eyes wide open — and just said "Sorry" and continued walking. She continued berating me, and most probably stayed angry long after this incident happened. Instead of just riding around a lost pedestrian, she made the situation deeply unsatisfying for her.

Such incidents occur quite frequently in Germany. People will drive slowly on purpose and honk at you because you've overtaken them, and accidentally queue-jumping in a supermarket puts the cat among the pigeons. Here, adherence and directness merge, making a confrontational and aggressive impression to foreigners. Finally, all of these lead to angry people and a bad mood in the air (see Chapter 3, "Perception of the culture").

Another form of "because I'm right" is the love for facts and figures, especially figures. "How much cheese did you buy for dinner?" *Quite a bit, a lot, not so much, less than last time* — these are not the kind of replies you'll hear. In Germany, it's more like — *four pieces, 250 grams, 500 grams* — figures that represent a clear value with no room for ambiguity and interpretation.

In some situations, the appreciation for figures can give off a kind of "know-it-all" impression. For example:

Li Wei explained: "It took us four hours yesterday to reach Dortmund. This was at least a 150-kilometer drive."

"No, from Cologne to Dortmund it's 95 kilometers," Helmut replied.

Chatmanee stated: "I read in the newspaper that Mercedes is most probably the biggest car maker in Germany."

"No, this cannot be. Volkswagen is far bigger than Mercedes," Sebastian corrected.

Such statements come across as monotone and unemotional. You didn't break any written or unwritten rule, you were just wrong, and the replier corrected you with the intention of helping. Correcting someone is customary in Germany and not perceived as offensive by Germans. And in general, nothing is wrong with a valid correction. What irritates foreigners is first, the harsh tone — "No, this is wrong", "No, it's…" usually starting with a "No" — and second, Germans correct you in front of others. In relationship-oriented cultures, you would expect a reply as follows:

> Chatmanee stated: "I read in the newspaper that Mercedes is most probably the biggest car maker in Germany."
> "Oh yes, interesting," Sebastian replied. "Mercedes is very big and famous in Germany. For sure, it's one of the top three car makers. I'm not sure which is first currently, Volkswagen or Mercedes."

Don't take offense at the "know-it-all" behavior. People want to help you, and offering facts and figures and aiming to correct are deeply rooted in the German culture. You can use the standard reply: "Oh, interesting. I didn't know that."

Finally, there is one big exception when it comes to adherence. It's the traffic on the German highway, called the "Autobahn." Of course, there is no comparison to be made to traffic violations in other countries, but for German standards, the people violate the rules quite frequently. They exceed the speed limit, tailgate, and overtake in the wrong lane. That's common practice on German highways. If you're new to the Autobahn, I suggest you follow the rules even if others don't.

📋 Chapter Summary

- Bureaucracy, rules, and regulations are highly valued.
- People are used to following rules and regulations, and so should you.
- Your status and personal connections will not speed up a process.
- Germans are not risk takers, and don't expect flexibility or spontaneous decisions.
- Accept that Germans protect and defend their position.
- Don't be offended by the "know-it-all" behavior.

Chapter 5

Key Characteristic #3 — Commitment and Early Warning

As Germans have a fact-oriented culture, they plan activities on a very detailed level. Actually, Germans love planning. They come up with task lists, set deadlines, and schedule appointments way in advance. Maintaining schedules and meeting deadlines means that you are reliable, and reliability is one of the German core values. Tardiness and ignoring deadlines means that you are not reliable. And once you are deemed as not reliable, you are watermarked. And I'm not just talking about milestones in major projects; this also applies to simple and small commitments you make. If you tell your business partner "I will call you tomorrow" and you don't call them, they will remember it, no matter whether the call was important or not.

When a meeting is scheduled at 4:30 p.m., then it means that you need to show up at 4:30 p.m. exactly, not 4:40 p.m. or 4:35 p.m. Arriving two or three minutes late is acceptable. But longer delays will annoy the organizer of the meeting. So, try to be punctual for meetings. This applies especially to telephone conferences. If you already know beforehand that you can't make it to the meeting on time, inform the organizer that you will be late.

THE MISSING REPORT

Richard Wong worked for a Singaporean Information Technology consulting firm and led a project team in Germany. Once a month, Richard traveled to Hamburg to meet his German client for a status meeting. During a meeting one month, they discussed a small issue in one of the software modules. Richard promised to analyze the issue and summarize his findings in a small report. "I will email the report to you by Thursday evening," he told his German business contact. The module was not of high importance and delivery was due in three months. As there were no other problems in the project, they closed the meeting and continued with their daily business.

Unfortunately, the next day, a critical incident popped up and Richard was fully engaged in fixing this problem. After a 20-hour work day, with great dedication and effort from Richard and his team, they successfully remedied the issue — without any impact on the German client's business.

A few days later, Richard called his German business partner. Proud of the positive result, he gave him a status update about successfully fixing the issue.

"OK," replied the client, "I can confirm that there's been no impact on the business... But what about the report from the last status meeting? You agreed to send it by Thursday, and I still haven't received it!"

Richard was baffled; his team had done an amazing job and all he'd heard was, "Where is this damned report!"

So, what went wrong? For the German client, the resolving of the incident was "as expected." "That's what they paid for," so to say. But as for the report, Richard made a commitment: He promised to deliver it by Thursday. Even though the report was not important at all, Richard had failed to honor a commitment, and that was unacceptable for his German client.

Richard did everything right in this case: He had to fix the serious issue first and then start on the report afterwards. He just missed one very important thing in Germany: Early warning. Germans will accept you missing or postponing a deadline, or even canceling a commitment, as long as you inform them early enough. If Richard had called the client on Wednesday evening or even Thursday morning and apologized that he couldn't deliver the report on time, then the client would have accepted that without any complaints. The client was well aware that the critical incident was of far higher importance than the report on a small module.

Early warnings are very important in Germany. You won't lose face if you give an early warning and announce a delay. But you will damage your reputation if you say nothing and ignore the commitment. This is a major difference between Germany and other cultures. As mentioned in "Chapter 3: Key Characteristic #1 — Directness," no feedback means everything is running as expected. But if you foresee problems, communicate them; and communicate them early enough.

The Asian habit of saying "yes" at once to most things causes trouble in Germany. When a German makes a proposal and asks, "Do you agree?", Asian people often respond with "Yes" immediately. But actually, they don't really agree; they just mean, "Yes, I have understood the proposal and will think about it." But the German takes that first "yes" as a commitment: "Yes, I accepted the proposal." The German won't further discuss this topic because they think it's closed. So it will cause irritation if, after a while, you raise concerns or even disagree with the proposal. When you've been asked a simple "yes or no" question, before responding, take a short pause, think about it, and then answer. Your first answer is taken into account. And if you're still not sure whether to respond "yes" or "no," simply say, "I can't make a decision yet. I'll have to think about it."

Communication Structure

Sentences are structured differently in direct cultures and indirect cultures. Indirect cultures avoid confrontation; hence they start to describe the context first before addressing the issue, usually in a subtle way. For example:

> Wai Lee reported: "We are now aligning the project components, and all teams should deliver the containers to Keppel Terminal. The terminal office has already provided the space and is ready. Our communication with the terminal guys is fine so far. Our basement team has all the items loaded into a container and it's ready for shipping. The construction equipment team is on the way, ready for shipping, which should be achieved tomorrow. I think both teams did a great job. The building structure team hasn't delivered yet, but I guess they'll be ready for shipping by the end of next week."

The actual issue — late delivery by the building structure team — is mentioned as the last item after a whole lot of other things. Direct cultures address the issue head on, and add context-related descriptions afterwards. For example:

> Christian said: "Where is the building structure team? The delivery date is today, and they haven't even provided a status report. The Keppel guys can't keep the space forever. We need to make sure the building structure team delivers as soon as possible. The containers from the basement and equipment teams are useless without the structure team. How can I help?"

These contrasting ways of communicating are instilled in an individual since childhood; you can't just change from one to the other. There are two major challenges here:

1) People from indirect cultures perceive you addressing an issue straight on as an "in-your-face" approach. They'll switch into defensive mode, either aggressively blaming you or ceasing communication.

2) People from direct cultures listen first while you explain the context. But after a short while, their minds begin to wander as they only hear "blah blah blah," and they ask themselves, "What's the problem?" Once you finally get to the problem, people from direct cultures don't really hear it, as their thoughts are somewhere else.

These two differing ways of communicating cause plenty of intercultural misunderstandings. People from the indirect culture think that they clearly stated the issue but nobody took it seriously. People from the direct culture don't even understand that there is a problem. However, there will come a point in time when the problem becomes obvious, and suddenly they will complain, "Why didn't you tell me earlier?"

It's not easy to change these communication styles, as they are deeply wired by a person's heritage. To handle the contrast, I suggest making it conscious. Before going into the conversation, remind yourself of these differences. Do it before every meeting, every presentation, and every bilateral talk.

Keep the Information Flow Going

In today's global organizations, the majority of communication is via email or instant messaging. Written text is a great source for intercultural misunderstandings, and I could fill a book on this topic alone. Here is one example emphasizing email replies:

SILENCE IS GOLDEN. ISN'T IT?

Anna — a German engineer — was working with colleagues in the United States (US) and she asked for their help extending an existing service provided by the US team. The company's standard data-transfer bandwidth was too small to cope with transferring a huge file between Europe and US, and Anna initiated a meeting to discuss a one-time bandwidth extension. The US team listened actively to the proposal, and promised to look into it and let Anna know whether it could be done. A week later, Anna hadn't received any answer, so she wrote an email and asked for a follow-up. A week later, she still had no answer, so she asked for a status update. She received no answer at all.

Anna was upset. She couldn't understand how, when they all had attended a meeting and agreed on the next steps, the US team wasn't doing anything. At least, that was the impression Anna had.

On the other side, in US, the team had already done the analysis on the first day and found out that the bandwidth extension could be done easily. Without further ado, the team jumped on it and started the implementation. The whole team had put in a lot of effort — including overtime — and they were proud that they would be able to deliver a working solution within a couple of weeks.

Two different views on the same thing: the US team, who worked hard to get the job done, and Anna, thinking these guys didn't give a hoot and couldn't even be bothered to write an email. The problem here was that the US team didn't send an update. Anna expected first, the outcome of the analysis, and second, a weekly status update in case the work could be done.

It's important in Germany to keep the information flow going. No matter whether the proposed work can be done or not, communicate with your business partner. If you have no new information, also communicate this. It's perfectly fine to say that you are still looking into the proposal but need more time. Just communicate.

The strictest commitment you can make is to sign a contract. Be very careful before signing a contract in Germany: They are legally binding and not just "guidelines" for a business partnership. Each sentence is interpreted exactly as it's written down in the contract. If you break a clause, you'll most probably be chased by your contract partner and end up paying severe penalties. In particular, price negotiations are a sensitive point. A fixed price is a fixed price. It's difficult — if not impossible — to raise the price after a contract is signed. Make sure you consider all the details and possible repercussions before signing a contract.

Chapter Summary

- Honor your commitments.
- When you make a commitment, treat it seriously, no matter whether it's for business or private life.
- If you foresee that you will not be able to deliver on a commitment, give your counterpart an early warning, before the commitment is due.
- You won't lose face if you give an early warning, but you will damage your reputation if you ignore the commitment.
- If you have no new information, communicate that you have no new information.
- Keep the different communication styles of indirect and direct cultures in mind.
- Once signed, contracts are binding.

Chapter 6

Non-Service

So far, we have covered the most important points that will help you in your daily interaction with Germans: directness, adherence, and commitment. However, there is another feature you can observe during your spare time in Germany, either as a businessperson or a tourist: the unique "experience" of customer service (better termed "non-service") in restaurants and service industries.

Many countries have a service-oriented society: most Asian countries, North America, and even some European countries that are tourist-oriented, such as Austria and Portugal — in these countries, the customer is always right. Always? No, not in Germany. In Germany, we have a kind of non-service-oriented society. What do I mean by "non-service?"

A TOURIST IN MUNICH

My first tourist place in Munich was, of course, the famous Hofbräuhaus.[1] I found a nice spot in the beer garden outside and I wanted to order a mass[2] of beer, but there was no waitress. I waited

---

(Continued)

---

[1] Website of the Hofbraeuhaus in Munich, the original one: http://www. hofbraeuhaus.de.

[2] "Mass" is a German word for a mug that holds 1 liter of beer. It's popular in southern Germany, especially in beer gardens and the Oktoberfest.

(Continued)

— 5 minutes... 10 minutes... 15 minutes — still no waitress. So, I decided to move to the bar and collect a mass of beer by myself.

The barman immediately told me, "You can't get a beer by yourself. You need to have a seat at a table."

"I do have a seat," I replied. "I've already waited for 15 minutes, and there's been no waitress in sight."

"Fifteen minutes?" he asked, surprised. "That's not very long. Just take a seat and the waitress will come."

Amazed, I went back to my seat, and after waiting another ten minutes, I left the restaurant and decided to try my luck elsewhere.

In the next restaurant — a rustic Bavarian place — the situation was much better. There was a waitress serving guests, but serving the other guests only, not me. I don't know what I did wrong, but she passed my table at least five times, and even though we made eye contact, she didn't ask for my order. After fifteen minutes, on the sixth time she passed my table, I finally managed to place my order. She made no apology for the long wait; it seemed to be quite normal there.

However, I couldn't really blame the waitress. There were 20 to 30 tables in the beer garden fully occupied by customers, but only one waitress. So, the waitress was working flat out, and people had to wait 15 to 20 minutes to place an order. In India or China, a restaurant of the same size would have a waiting staff of at least five, if not ten, to serve the customers.

This kind of situation won't arise in each restaurant or shop. But if it occurs, don't be annoyed or upset when you find service personnel acting this way. There are also shops and restaurants that provide good service. It's just that sometimes you won't feel like a valued customer, but more like an annoying suppliant. When you face such a situation, and you will, just keep being friendly and relaxed, and try to get your purchase done or move on to the next place.

EFFECTIVE COMMUNICATION

Once, I entered a bakery and asked, "Do you have wholemeal bread?"
"No!" was the quick answer.
"Will you get some today?" was my next question.
"No, it's already sold out," said the sales assistant, and moved on to the next customer.

Sure, the assistant was right, they had no wholemeal bread anymore, and the quickest, most efficient way to communicate that was to say, "No." Two characters; the word couldn't be shorter. In Japan or the United States, you would expect a reply like, "I'm very sorry, but we're out of wholemeal bread today. The next delivery won't arrive before tomorrow morning. Would you care for sunflower-seed bread instead?" In Germany, you get "No" — directness combined with non-service.

Shopping

Shopping experiences during my first visit to Taiwan made a lasting impression on me. As soon as I entered a small shop, the assistant came up to me and asked how I was and how she could help. After replying that I was fine and that I was just looking around, she kept at my side, following me throughout the shop — unusual and a bit hassling for me, as I wasn't used to it. I prefer to walk around freely and ask when I need help. Later, I learned from a Taiwanese friend that her behavior was typical. An assistant must be ready whenever needed, especially when the customer is the only person in the shop.

In Germany, conversely, you feel unnoticed in a shop. It seems like the assistants ignore you. There are cases where they do indeed ignore you, but often, the assistants just want to give you privacy and avoid bothering or hassling you. Feel free to walk around and ask an assistant as soon as you need help. That's the shopping experience that Germans expect. Though finding an available assistant is often a challenge in crowded shops. Labor costs are high, and you see this especially in the service industry: busy shops with more than twenty customers, but just two or three assistants to serve them.

Supermarkets also have their own style of service. On a busy Friday evening, you'll notice long queues in front of the cash registers, ten people or more waiting their turn. However, it's unbelievable how fast the cashiers scan the goods, take the money, and issue the receipts. Compared to cashiers in somewhere like Singapore or Thailand, the cashiers in Germany are at least three times faster. The whole process is well organized; hence a queue of six to ten people clears considerably quickly. But on the downside, the speed of the process also depends on your actions — nobody opens a bag for you and puts your goods into it; you do this all by yourself. And if you aren't used to this, it can get stressful. As you take your purchases and put them in a bag, the next customer's shopping is already being processed. Be quick with your packing, or you'll cause a jam and earn "the look" from the other customers!

Other "features" you might observe in German supermarkets are:

- A deposit of 50 cents is required to use a shopping cart. This should ensure a customer returns the cart where it should be returned, and doesn't leave it somewhere else.
- Goods are not on shelves, they're on pallets still in the shipping cardboard boxes. In some cases, you have to open the cardboard first before taking the product. This is especially common at discount supermarkets.
- Plastic bags aren't free; they cost about 10–25 cents.
- Shop assistants are difficult to find. Sometimes just one or two are on duty for the whole market. If you find one, they're usually busy restocking the shelves and aren't happy to answer questions.

Service is simply not a priority in German supermarkets. The nationwide supermarket chains focus on product variety, good quality, and a competitive price (often the cheapest in Europe). German customers have complained about the service, but generally they've gotten used to it and accept it, as long the price is OK. If they have to decide between the price and service, without hesitating for a second, they will choose the price.

And there are plenty more bad services out there: telecommunication companies (the worst), airlines, taxi drivers, consumer hotlines, public transport, etc. Yet it wouldn't be fair to list all the culprits here, as they exist globally — especially taxi drivers. When I started to write this book a couple of years ago, I planned to dedicate a section for the grumpy taxi drivers in Munich. Meanwhile, as I traveled multiple times across different countries, I can confirm that Munich taxi drivers aren't worse than taxi drivers anywhere else. At least they switch on the meter every time without asking and charge the proper standard fare.

In recent years, service standards have been improving, especially in the area of online shopping. Due to strong competition from global companies like Amazon and IKEA, which adore service, German companies have been forced to react and raise their standards, or they risk losing customers.

There is a positive aspect of service (or non-service) in Germany: Wherever you go, whatever you buy, whichever service you use, you can trust that the service providers are honest and treat everybody equally. You pay the same price for a product or service as a local and as a visitor.

Queuing Strategy

When you shop in bakeries or other small shops, it will catch your eye that there is no visible queue. All the customers stand in a crowd in front of the sales counter, and the assistant asks, "Who's next?"

In fact, there is a queue; it's just a kind of unofficial queue. You have to remember who was first and when it will be your turn. If you pushed in, you will be advised by some other customer to wait your turn; sometimes in a friendly way, sometimes not. But rest assured, you will be advised. Queue-jumping is considered very impolite in Germany and can cause aggressive comments from bystanders.

Finally, it's important to know that you will notice such behaviors only in your spare time. You won't encounter impolite or unfriendly behavior when working with German colleagues. In work relationships, the communication style is polite. In spite of all the directness, German people are polite and friendly in business when talking to each other.

Chapter Summary

- Service is an ambiguous concept in Germany. Don't expect the service you are used to in Asia or US.
- Due to high labor costs, the number of service personnel is kept to a minimum.
- If service is not as you expected, just keep being friendly and relaxed and try to get your purchase done.
- Service staffs are honest and treat everybody equally (badly).
- In work relationships, communication is polite.

Chapter 7

Business Subjects

Now that we've covered the three key characteristics, let's have a look at other German behaviors. In this chapter, I've summarized topics that will crop up in your day-to-day business with German colleagues or business partners. Topics like exaggeration, feedback, expectations, and understanding business titles may be minor, but they can have a big impact on your daily work.

The main focus is on business topics, but you can also find helpful information here for visiting Germany as a tourist, such as details on gifts, corruption, and flattery.

Exaggeration in Presentations

After working for a German company for a couple of years, I went to work for a United States (US) company. Obviously, I expected a different working style, especially when it came to communication. The US company was a glitzy multinational company headquartered in Silicon Valley with more than 100,000 employees. The directors held presentations in the lobby of the headquarters and live-streamed them for a global audience, so that every employee could watch these meetings live. Most of these meetings followed the same agenda:

1. Welcoming the audience
2. Introduction

3. Talking about the topic
4. Question and Answer (Q&A)

Welcoming the audience usually involved phrases like "It's so amazing that you're here today," "I'm so grateful to be speaking to such an excellent audience," "Today I'm going to tell you something about the greatest thing that's ever happened in this great company," or simply, "Fantastic!" When ending the meeting with a Q&A, every question from an attendee was first acknowledged with, "Thank you, that's a GREAT question" (really, *every* question). In my first year with the US company, I heard the words "fantastic" and "awesome" more often than in the entire 10-year period I'd been in Germany.

How were these meetings perceived by the company's branch in Munich, Germany? In general, Germans saw the welcome statements as completely exaggerated. When somebody announces "the greatest thing that's ever happened in this company," Germans expect something like a huge acquisition, or a new partnership of equals, or an increase in the revenue forecast of 30% — not things like an individual contributor winning an award or the introduction of a new internal communications platform. You can imagine the disappointment of the German colleagues when such things were communicated after announcing them as "the greatest thing." After a while, the German teams got used to these exaggerated terms and even made fun of them, calling the new coffee machine "a fantastic, influential investment that will shape the future of the company."

When presenting to a German audience, don't use overstatements — even if these statements are perfectly normal in your culture. When you announce "the greatest thing" in Germany, you should feel comfortable that this really is the game changer that the audience will expect.

Similarly, consider the Germans' perception of "this is a great question" during the Q&A. Some questions may really be great, but most of them were pretty standard. There's no need to call a question like "What's the revenue outlook for the next quarter?" a "great question." Germans usually reply with, "Thanks for the question," or answer the question on the spot without acknowledging it. Again, the reply for the "great question" was perceived as ridiculously over the top by Germans, and ended up as a running gag:

"Mike, do you want to join me for a coffee?"
"Thanks, Robert, that's a GREAT question."

Asking for Feedback

Another common theme in US presentations is encouraging the audience to give feedback after the meeting. The presenter would go through the agenda and talk about specific topics. Then he or she would say, "Please contact Person A or Person B if you have any further questions or want to give feedback," "Don't hesitate to contact Ann to give feedback," or "We want to improve consistently and to do so, we rely on your valuable feedback." Sounds great.

This is done in Germany too. There, I gave feedback in such cases, and it was acknowledged and appreciated. Even if the recipient of the feedback was a C-Level executive, I got a personalized reply. So, when the directors at the US company asked for feedback multiple times during presentations, and even provided their personal email addresses in order to receive feedback, I took that as a clear communication that feedback would be highly appreciated. I gave feedback on various topics, like presentation style and content. But not once did I receive a reply: no acknowledgement, no thank you, not even a note that the feedback had been received, let alone a personal response.

This was a disappointment to me, as it was to my German colleagues. And worse, it would be the last time the company received feedback, because they failed to acknowledge it. Even if you don't agree with the feedback, it's important that you at least acknowledge it and thank the person giving the feedback.

Flattery

Some cultures have perfectly mastered the art of flattery — US and India — just to name two. In both countries, it's part of daily business to compliment your counterpart. "You're looking great today," "Wow, your dress is amazing," "You did a brilliant job today," "Your results were perfect," "Tremendous performance." Most of such comments are made when someone did quite a normal job, nothing special. But it's part of these cultures to communicate this way.

Flattery is quite unusual in Germany. Germans would see these phrases as exaggerations, and would wonder, *what does this person really want when they're flattering me so much? There must be a hidden agenda.* On the other side, don't expect such flattery from Germans. As already mentioned in Chapter 3: "Giving feedback," Germans give positive acknowledgements on quite a subtle level. When complimenting Germans, take care to do it subtly.

Gifts

It's not common in Germany to give gifts, not even in the first getting-to-know-you meetings. However, if you do so, it's certainly appreciated. The gift should reflect your background; for example, it can be something from your home country or specific culture. Keep the cost of the gift low (see the next section) — anything below 50 Euros is fine. You only need to wrap gifts for special events like Christmas or birthdays. And don't be surprised if you hand over a wrapped gift and it's opened immediately right in front of you. This is the culture. In case you receive a wrapped gift, also open it immediately. The giver will be irritated if you don't open it right after receiving it.

Corruption

In short, corruption is more or less nonexistent. Once in a while, the media reports on high-profile corruption cases involving politicians or multinational corporations. These are rare cases, and when they do happen, they're beaten to death by the tabloids.

Whether you're working with a business partner; visiting a government office; dealing with the police; negotiating with someone in a service industry, in a civil or a private situation; bribery will not speed up the process. On the contrary, you can be quite sure that even an attempt to bribe someone will lead to a complain of criminal activity.

To prevent the slightest chance of any corruption, some town councils — like Munich — passed a bill that prohibits garbage collectors from taking tips in cash. At least non-monetary gifts up to a specific limit are allowed, so these hard-working guys are allowed to take Christmas cookies without committing a crime.

A reminder to any foreigner visiting Germany regarding bribes: Hands off!

Greetings

During my time in Regensburg, I worked for a German manu-facturing company. In 2006 the company expanded their facility in Penang, and trainees from Malaysia visited Regensburg for on-the-job training. A Chinese project manager joined our group and was based in our office for a couple of weeks. Usually, he arrived at the office around 8 a.m. and went straight to his desk without saying a word. It's not that I'm fond of somebody greeting me personally when entering the office, but saying nothing felt strange. Only then did it come to my attention that at least saying "Morning" when entering the office is standard conduct in Germany. Later on, it turned out that the other team members in the office perceived our colleague's conduct in the same way. Quickly, the Chinese guy got a reputation of "*Der kann nicht grüßen,*" which means that he hadn't been trained to greet people.

It's considered proper business conduct to greet colleagues when entering your office with at least a "Morning" or "Hello."

Expectation Management

Marketing products or services is part of the daily business of every vendor. In regular sales conversations, you highlight the benefits and focus on what's in it for the customer. However, salespeople tend to overstate the benefits. Globally, this is accepted as standard business practice, and most customers don't think that what's said in a sales pitch is carved in stone, but is more of a general description of the product and its benefits.

Say you tell a customer, "This printing machine is revolutionary. Nothing like this has been on the market before, and it will delight you. The cost is among the lowest of all printers on the market, if not the best of all." The customer will take this with a pinch of salt. In Germany, however, you need to be careful with such statements. Often they are taken literally, and if your product is not one of the cheapest on the market, or it's not as "revolutionary" as mentioned, you will be met with skepticism. You will still be able to sell your product, but the customer will dig deeper and try to understand what you mean by "revolutionary." You're better off using concrete facts to prove the benefits, instead of using general sales terms that are quite common in other parts of the world.

United States Sales Term	German Sales Term
Revolutionary	Revolutionary because it brews a cup of coffee in under one minute and uses only half of the coffee grounds.

(Continued)

Best car in its class on the market	Best car in the entry sedan segment, with the lowest fuel consumption (4.1 liters per 100 kilometers) and lowest CO_2 emissions (64g/km); Global Positioning System (GPS) as standard.
Healthiest yogurt in the nation	The only yogurt with 0.1% fat and less than 5 grams of sugar.
World-class search — find more with less effort	Compare 25 travel agencies at once, and find the cheapest flight within five seconds.
Your one-stop-shop for everything phone-related	Latest models with 20% discounts, 5G data plans less than 20 EUR per month, repairs, configurations, and upgrades — everything you need in one shop.

Other examples of poor expectation management can be found in sports. The year 2015 was a great one for the German soccer club "Bayern München." They headed the Bundesliga (the highest German soccer league) from the very beginning of the season, outplayed every other team, and won the league with a huge lead two months before the end of the season. As soon as it was certain that they'd won the league, the coach of Bayern München — Pep Guardiola, a Spaniard — made the statement, "Only the triple is enough." In soccer language "the triple" means winning the national league (Bundesliga), the national cup (DFB-Pokal), and the Champions League within a year — something only a handful of international soccer teams could achieve. After Bayern München won the Bundesliga, they competed against Borussia Dortmund to win the national cup. Bayern München lost in the penalty shootout. Two weeks later, they competed against FC Barcelona in the Champions League Semi-Finals, and Bayern München lost by 3:5. Meanwhile, they had reduced their efforts in the remaining Bundesliga matches to fully focus on the Champions League. Hence, they lost three consecutive games in the Bundesliga against weaker opponents.

After the season was finally over, the team — and especially the coach — was criticized for their efforts. Fans moaned even though the team played a great season, achieving an excellent Bundesliga victory and reaching the semi-finals in two important competitions. But five words from Pep Guardiola, "Only the triple is enough," set expectations to the highest possible level, despite the chance of success being small.

Be careful with your choice of words, no matter whether in competitions, businesses, or private lives. Manage expectations wisely.

Vacations

When working in Germany, you will notice that somebody is always on vacation. By law, every employee gets a minimum of 25 working days of vacation leave annually, and usually bigger companies grant their employees 30 days of paid vacation. Yes, 30 days; that's six weeks off. And vacation means traveling abroad or domestically, but definitely not being reachable for business matters. Vacation time is taken seriously in Germany; in general, people highly value their private life and keep it separate from their everyday working life. Don't try to reach German colleagues for work matters during their vacation. Unless it's a real emergency, interrupting a vacation is considered impolite.

In US, employees are given between eight and eighteen days of paid vacation leave per year.[1] However, when I joined my first US company, I was surprised by how many people were on sabbatical. It turned out that the US company grants their employees four weeks of sabbatical for every four years of service, or eight weeks

---

[1] Paid vacation days in the US: https://www.bls.gov/news.release/ebs.t05.htm.

accumulated for every seven years of service. So, a sabbatical was either four or seven weeks off work, which would be considered a longer vacation in Germany. The term "sabbatical" is also used in Germany, but in general it means being off work for at least six months, and commonly one year.

Business Titles

Germans mean what they say, and this applies to business titles. In other cultures, titles on business cards may not be well defined and could mean anything. When working with Asian cultures, like Indian and Chinese people, I can't remember seeing a business card that didn't include the words "senior" or "manager." It's different in Germany. There isn't a clearly defined specification or rule; however, business titles are used similarly in medium-sized to large companies. For example, in a MNC with more than 20,000 employees, a business title structure like this is common:

Business Title	Management Level	Experience/Leadership
Engineer/Analyst	Individual contributor	<5 years of experience
Senior Engineer/ Analyst	Individual contributor	5–10 years of experience
Staff Engineer/ Analyst	Individual contributor	>10 years of experience
Manager	First-line manager	leading a team of 3–15 people
Senior Manager	Middle management	leading a team of 5–20 people
Director	Middle management	leading a team of 20–50 people

(Continued)

(Continued)

Senior Director	Upper management	leading a team >50 people
Vice President	Top management	leading a whole business group or a part of it
Executive/ Corporate VP	Top management	leading a whole business group
President	CEO	

Positions from senior director onwards are usually considered "Leitender Angestellter" (executive employee), which means that they have a special work contract outside of any tariff boundaries and less restrictive legal boundaries regarding social security and workers' protection.

These rules and titles are not written in stone, but are general guidelines for what to expect from business titles in Germany and the people behind them.

When handing over a business card to someone, you need no special conduct. Contrary to other cultures, it doesn't matter whether you give the card with both hands or single-handedly.

Dress Code

Dress code in Germany depends on the industry or organization. In general, business attire is on the casual side. Suits and ties are common only in the banking, legal, and insurance industries. Also, salespeople usually wear a suit and tie. In most other organizations, a business-casual dress code is common for the senior management staff (vice president and above). However, in many companies — including MNCs — even senior managers don't wear a suit. Casual dress code is absolutely fine and accepted for nearly all business conducts.

For your first contact I suggest you wear a jacket, and then in subsequent meetings, continue with whatever you feel comfortable wearing. As long as you avoid obvious faux pas, like shorts, sandals, or shabby clothing, you can't go wrong.

Role of the Manager

The dominant management style in Germany is collaboration, where the managers of teams have a collaborative partner role. They listen to the opinions of the team members and make decisions together with the team members. Their main job is to define the organization's direction while details are worked out by the team.

Contrary to the Indian and Chinese leadership styles, managers don't necessarily know all the details of their organization. It isn't seen as negative if managers admit that they don't know a specific subject but suggest contacting a member of their team to get a detail clarified.

It's also fine to speak up or suggest a proposal before the manager has voiced an opinion. An open discussion — even criticizing a manager's proposal — is no problem, and in many companies, it's even encouraged that employees speak openly and bring issues to the table. Conflicts are resolved head-on. Managers act like moderators within the teams, but they commonly get hands-on if the situation requires it.

Note that — unlike some Asian cultures — an open office door doesn't mean that employees are invited to view documents on the manager's desk. Managers just leave the door open to encourage people to talk to them anytime.

Tariff, Unions, and Workers' Protection

Workers' rights protection in Germany is one of the strongest in the world, with strict labor laws supervised by government bodies. For instance, in most sectors the total working hours on a single day must not exceed 10 hours. Also, in most sectors, Germans are not allowed to work on Sundays. For exceptions, the company needs to get written approval from the regulating authority beforehand.

For large companies, it's common to partner with nationwide labor unions. Doing so is not required by law — a company can choose to opt out of an association of unions — but in general, companies try to keep a good relationship with them.

Irrespective of whether a company is a member of an association or not, its employees can install a local workers' council as soon the company has more than five employees.[2] The size of the council depends on the size of the company:

Company Size	Workers' Council Size
5–21 employees	Single person doing council tasks in addition to their job duties
22–200 employees	Several people doing council tasks in addition to their job duties
More than 200 employees	One or more dedicated people doing only council tasks

The workers' council consists of elected employees who represent the concerns of the whole workforce to the company's management committee. They also maintain a close relationship with unions. Whenever a company has more than a single location, each site can set up a workers' council of their own. In cases where more than one workers' councils are installed, an overall company workers' council must be set up. So, a manager may need to talk to multiple councils over the same issue, such as a global reorganization.

---

[2] Betriebsverfassungsgesetz (BetrVG), summary: https://www.gesetze-im-internet.de/englisch_betrvg/index.html

One result of the three-strong forces — labor law, unions, and workers' councils — is plenty of regulatory documents called "Betriebsvereinbarung" (shop-floor agreements) that define all kind of work-related regulations. Examples are:

- Definition of work hours
- Handling of overtime work and on-call duty
- Privacy regulations
- Workplace ergonomic rules
- Company salary structure
- Employee benefits
- Performance review and promotion process
- Vacation regulations
- Termination process

In Germany it's quite difficult to fire people without having a really good reason, and just poor performance is not considered one. An employee must have been cited for multiple misconducts in the past, and have received written notices for those, before the termination process can be initiated, and usually it still takes a couple of months to complete. It starts with the written notices, and moves on to a corrective action plan with close follow-up by the employee and the manager. Then, a termination of employment requires the approval of the workers' council, and it often ends up with a decent package for the employee once they finally leave.

At work, approval is required for everything. Things like hiring new people, organizational changes, weekend work, and the introduction of information technology applications all require the workers' council approval. In some instances, even changing an individual's job title requires approval.

In many companies every employee has an individual work contract ("Arbeitsvertrag") that defines their working hours, salary structure, vacation allowance, benefits, terms of notice, job title, and so on. These contracts are signed by the employee and a representative of the company, usually someone from the human resources department.

In your day-to-day work with German colleagues, keep in mind that somebody is always on vacation (see the earlier section, "Vacation"), and you could end up in situations where people have to leave the company after ten hours of work. You can politely check on this first when you start your day. If you plan a half-nighter, ask your teammates how long are they available for today. They will tell you directly if they have to leave after 10 hours. Nowadays, when companies reduce automated work-time registration, you might also hear "open end" as an answer. Just clarify beforehand, to avoid being the only one in the office after 7 p.m.

Small Talk

As mentioned in Chapter 3, small talk is not of much importance when doing business with Germans. However, at parties, on vacation, or at informal gatherings, Germans do talk about non-work-related topics. Here it's important to understand what topics to talk about and what is best not to talk about. The following topics are safe bets to get a conversation going:

- Cars: Germans love cars! Germany is the country with the most upper-class car manufacturers in the word. BMW, Audi, Mercedes, and Porsche all have their headquarters in Germany. Additionally, you can find some mid-class manufacturers like Volkswagen and Opel. Get the conversation going with the famous "Autobahn," the local term for highway, and the fact that there are no speed limits in many sections. Or talk about driving culture in general: how safe it is, and whether people follow the rules or not. Driving is one of the few areas where Germans break the given rules and limits. "What car are you driving?", "How much is a BMW 3

Series here?", or, "Do people really drive 200 kilometers per hour (125 miles per hour)?" (Yes, they do!) are good starters.

- Food: As with every other culture, food is a perfect topic to stimulate a lively talk. Show that you did your homework and read up on German food beforehand. However, note that the typical German items like Weisswurst, Schnitzel, Breze, and Schweinshaxn are not as widespread as you might think. Many of them originated in Bavaria, where these dishes are still eaten regularly today. People in other parts of Germany don't eat Weisswurst at all. Ask what the typical local foods are in the area where you're currently staying, and which people prefer.

- Sports (especially soccer): Germany is a multiple world champion in soccer. Germans are proud of the national team and support their league teams in the international Champions League competition (a league where the top teams of each European country compete for the number-one spot in Europe). The German league "Bundesliga" consists of some of the top players and coaches in the world, and is getting more and more attention globally. The Bundesliga — like the English Premier League — is followed throughout Asia; teams like Bayern München and Borussia Dortmund are known in China, Malaysia, and Japan. Other popular sports are cross-country skiing, Formula 1, and tennis. By the way, if you want to end a conversation politely, start to talk about cricket or baseball, two internationally well-known sports that are more or less nonexistent in Germany — the German you're speaking to will soon get bored and make an excuse to leave.

- Vacations and travel: "German travelers are everywhere", so they say. Traveling is the number-one favorite pastime (no surprise there, with 30 days of vacation time). Ask Germans where they spent their last holiday and they will rave about their vacation spots. Destinations are spread across domestic regions, Europe, and other continents. Germany itself offers plenty of places to visit.

Beside the main cities — Munich, Berlin, and Hamburg — and the well-known spots — Neuschwanstein Castle and Koenigssee — there are plenty of other options to explore the wonderful country: Erzgebirge, Saechsche Schweiz, Schwarzwald, Allgaeu, or along the Danube river are all pleasant nature areas.

- Hobbies: In addition to the number-one hobby — traveling — there are also popular pastimes. Germans are proud of their hobbies. Many of them do individual sports, such as cycling, hiking in the mountains, and running; others enjoy activities such as gardening and do-it-yourself home improvement. In general, do-it-yourself is the mantra when it comes to work in the household. (Traditionally, Germans try to fix broken things on their own before calling a skilled worker. This is driven by the high labor costs: A one-hour handyman visit can easily cost more than 100 Euros.) An interested "What are your favorite hobbies?" question is always well received.

As there are topics that are great to get the conversation going with Germans, there are also others that can lead to awkward situations and should be avoided:

- Anything related to World War II (and World War I, for that matter): This is the most sensitive topic in Germany. Germans have a strained relationship with World War II. They accept that they were the aggressors during this historical period, and they are doing everything they can to prevent re-emerging Nazi tendencies. This shows up sometimes in strange reactions when a non-German resident in the country commits a crime and nobody emphasizes that they are foreign in case it is seen as an anti-immigrant sentiment. Talking about key World War II aggressors such as Hitler, Goebbels, and Himmler are frowned upon. To praise such individuals results in a jail term or at least a trial. Dealing — or even showing off — Nazi artifacts is a criminal offense. Avoid anything World War related at all costs.

- Race: Germany has had issues with racist attacks by Neo-Nazis in the past, and other parts of the country were overrun by refugees. Some of the refugees committed crimes, causing upheaval in the community. The media is traditionally "left-wing" oriented and downplayed those incidents. Politics and some communities are more on the "right wing," and this discrepancy often leads to heated discussions.

- Salary: There are cultures and countries where you can talk openly about salary. Not in Germany: Salary is one of the best-kept secrets there. Virtually nobody knows how much even their closest colleagues earn for the same job. People believe that an open salary structure leads to a culture of jealousy and hence they keep the figures under wraps. You should follow this rule and not ask people how much they earn. General salary questions like "How much does a shop assistant usually earn?" are fine.

- Religion: The German calendar has many Christian and Catholic holidays; however, the population is not very religious. Some regions are more religious than others, but far less than 50% of the population take religion seriously. Also, superstition does not really exist. Sure, some people may consider "13" an unlucky number, for example, but actually nobody cares if a phone number ends with a thirteen, a double-four, or a triple-eight. Hence talking about religious or superstition topics should be avoided, or you may cause awkwardness. Don't talk about sects; they have a very bad reputation in the country. Even the term itself is associated with evil and with structures close to criminal organizations.

- Family: This isn't a topic that is specifically dangerous to address in Germany; it's just not like in Asian cultures, where it's normal to ask about the status of family — children, parents, family tree, and so on. Remember, Germans strictly separate private and business life. Once you get close to a German, it's not an issue to ask whether they are married or have children, their age, and so forth. Just avoid talking about private and family topics too early in the relationship.

Status Symbols

In a country with brands like Mercedes, BMW, Porsche, Montblanc, and Adidas, status must be of the utmost importance, right? Wrong. Sure, many people drive a BMW or Mercedes, but these brands are considered standard in Germany. If a German wants to show off, you can expect a Jaguar, Porsche, or Ferrari on the driveway.

But actually, showing off is frowned upon and considered bad manners. People have high standards in German society; they own nice cars and live in nice houses. That's it: Swim with the tide; no need to imply that you're better than others. Even if your status is evident in your private life — for example, you have a better car than your neighbor and clearly shows it — don't take this into your work environment, or you'll earn suspicious looks.

Many managers drive lower-class cars than their employees, and that's not a problem at all. I once had a senior director as a manager who led a team of more than 50 people, and he drove a 20-year-old car that was by far the oldest car of anyone in the organization. He didn't even hesitate to give colleagues a lift to company events in his car. There are no unwritten rules in Germany that a manager should (or must) have better things than the employees. The same goes for dress code: Keep it clean and tidy; no need to wear Armani, Versace, or Hugo Boss.

Forms of Address

Germany has a dual system for addressing people, formal and informal:

1. Informal:
   "Du": The equivalents of the English word "you," or included when addressing someone by the first name.
2. Formal:
   "Sie": There is no equivalent word in English; it's included when addressing someone by the last name.

In English, you always use "you." The distinction between formal and informal addressing is via the name. In Germany:

- When meeting someone you don't know (like a business partner, manager, or neighbor), I suggest using the formal address with the person's last name; for example, Ms. Braun. If the person likes to be addressed informally, she will say, "Call me Sophia."
- Peers usually address each other informally with the first name only (without Mr./Ms.): "Hi, Robert, how are you?" In informal environments, when you meet someone in a bar, during a celebration, or at a festival, you can address them by their first name.
- In MNCs, it's common to address someone by their first name even when meeting them for the first time. In case you are unsure, don't hesitate to ask: "How may I address you?"

Take the suggestions above as guidelines — there can be exceptions in other sectors. I've been in shops where salespeople who've worked together for years still address each other formally with "Sie" and the last name.

Chapter 8

Leisure Subjects

This chapter is about topics like shopping, dining, and entertainment. Here, I've focused primarily on tourists, but this chapter is also useful for businesspeople considering to spend time outside the office and explore the country. Take the information and recommendations here as guidelines and tips to help you better understand the German way of living. Note that this chapter just touches on subjects to give you a basic understanding; it's outside the scope of this book to take a comprehensive look at leisure subjects. To dig deeper into this area, I suggest reading a tourist guidebook.

Environmental Protection

Environmental care — covering climatic, nature, water, and health protection — is of utmost importance in Germany. There are strict regulations and controls on emissions from cars and industrial plants. Environmental protection spans business, public, and private areas — you'll find it nearly everywhere. It leads to great benefits; for example, due to strong controls, tap water in Germany is among the safest in the world — its quality in some regions exceeds the quality of off-the-shelf bottled water.

Environment protection results in a bunch of rules to follow, especially when it comes to garbage separation. Dividing trash into paper, plastic, glass (white color), glass (other colors), metal, fabric, and specific packaging can be confusing sometimes. However, the rules have been in place for years and everybody follows them strictly, and so should you.

To encourage people to return off-the-shelf bottles and cans to the shop instead of throwing them in the garbage bin, a deposit of 15–25 cents is added to the purchase price. This applies to glass and plastic bottles and the practice is quite cumbersome — many of the bottles can only be returned to the shop where you bought them. Bad luck for people who bought bottled drinks while traveling.

Some politicians complain that the whole system is too complex — not just for citizens but also for refuse processors to handle all the different types of garbage. Boroughs have started pilot schemes to reduce the separation required by improving the capabilities of automated separation machines. I look forward to seeing an easier system implemented in the future.

Shopping and Costs

Cost-wise, Germany is right in the middle: cheaper than Asian places, but more expensive than United States (US). This is especially so if you are a visitor from Asia or the Middle East, Germany is a great place to shop for branded goods. Designer clothing brands — Hugo Boss, Versace, Armani, to name but a few — are way cheaper, less than half the cost compared to Singapore, Bangkok, or Tokyo.

Another extremely cheap item is alcohol. In restaurants, half a liter of beer (which is the standard size in Bavaria) costs around 4 Euros; in a supermarket, it costs less than 1 Euro.

Supermarkets are among the cheapest in the world. You find all kinds of food for moderate prices with great sale offers. Huge competition exists between traditional supermarkets — which are already inexpensive — and the so-called "discounters," which are supermarkets with self-service and have a bare look and feel that brings prices down to an even lower level.

Interestingly, location doesn't make a big difference regarding the quality of food in Germany. You find great restaurants in tourist places and in remote places. The tourist restaurants in the city centers are well frequented by locals. The costs don't differ much: If you stick with German food, the price difference between a popular place in the city center and a restaurant in a suburb is no more than 30%. This is different to Asian cities like Bangkok, Mumbai, and Singapore, where the difference between a tourist and a local restaurant can easily be more than double, with no upwards limit. In Singapore, you can pay S\$4 for a plate of fried rice in a local restaurant, but you might pay S\$12 for the same dish in a tourist or expat spot.

Electronic products are competitively priced, but not so much that it's worth bringing them back overseas. Cars are quite cheap, due to low taxation and high competition. The huge number of German manufactured cars also leads to low prices on foreign cars. The overseas manufacturers keep the prices low to have a chance at competing with the same class car of German manufacturers.

Public transport is expensive for single trips. As soon as you take more than a couple of rides on suburban transport, it is more worthwhile to buy an all-day-ride ticket. For example, in Munich a 24-hour all-day-ride ticket costs about three times the price of a single ticket — starting from the fourth ride, you're better off buying the all-day-ride ticket. For long-distance transport, buy the ticket as early as possible. Purchasing the tickets a day or two before departure may lead to ridiculously expensive tickets; for example, more than 80 Euros for a three-hour trip. Domestic flights are in the moderate range (also depending on how early you book). Hotels in major cities are cheaper compared to other international cities.

When talking about costs, one word must be mentioned: *stingy*. Yes, Germans are as stingy as the Scottish. The reason status symbols aren't very important (see Chapter 7, "Status symbols") is that Germans are tight-fisted. In supermarkets, the cheapest products sell first. Invitations where the host pays for everything are rare, and tipping is evaluated carefully. Compared to people from other European countries, Germans are the least favored visitors; according to service staff like waiters, Germans tip the lowest amount.[1]

Shopping Hours

Shopping hours in Germany are unique to each state and vary across the country. In most states, malls and shops are open from 10 a.m. to 8 p.m.; some until 9 a.m. or 10 p.m. Note that on Sundays and public holidays, shops are closed everywhere. In some states, the local law allows "Shopping Sundays" every two to three months, where shops are open for a couple of hours, but that's rare and requires special permits. The strictest law applies in Bavaria, where all shops and supermarkets must be closed by 8 p.m., and on Sundays and public holidays, they must be closed all day with no exceptions.

In the background of these strict rules are the labor laws, unions, and employee protection (see "Tariff, unions, and workers' protection"). It's quite irritating to find the main tourist centers in Munich crowded with visitors on a sunny Sunday afternoon and yet every shop is closed. Historically, this is part of the German way of life, and it clearly shows that employee protection and private life come before revenue generation. The closed shops look abnormal to visitors, but locals are used to it. Though they do complain: Their issue isn't the closing time of 8 p.m., but that supermarkets start to close specific sections earlier. So, the veggie section may be closed by 7 p.m., or a bakery may stop selling coffee 30 minutes before closing time because "they've already cleaned the coffee machine."

---

[1] Welt online (2016): https://www.welt.de/reise/article155313788/Weshalb-Deutsche-bei-Kellnern-gefuerchtet-sind.html

Oktoberfest

First, the facts:

Oktoberfest is the world's largest traditional festival, and it runs every year for two weeks from a Saturday in mid-September (usually the third weekend) until the first Sunday in October. It's not held across Germany, but only in Munich at the Theresienwiese, an area of about 50 hectares (120 acres). It consists of three major areas:

1. The beer halls, which are called tents ("Zelte") by locals. However, these aren't real tents, they're more like huge wooden barracks that accommodate up to 8,000 people. Some of the beer halls also have an adjacent beer garden.
2. An outdoor area with food stalls and souvenir booths.
3. An amusement park with attractions for children and adults.

The festival attracts about six million visitors each year from all over the world. In a city of 1.5 million inhabitants, you can image that this amount of visitors pushes public places and transport to the limit. Hotels are fully booked months ahead, despite the prices being more than double during this period.

Second, the rules

During busy times (Friday evenings, public holiday evenings, Saturdays), entry to the beer halls is almost always closed, as they are overcrowded. You need a reservation to enter a hall during these times.

You need to make a reservation at least six months in advance, and the minimum booking is for one table (eight to ten people). A reservation for ten people costs about 250 Euros and includes vouchers for drinks and food.

During the week, you can find seats in a beer hall for a small group of two to three people if you arrive between 4 p.m. to 5 p.m.;

any later, it may be difficult. Bigger groups should arrive between 2 p.m. to 3 p.m. for a chance to find an empty table. If a beer hall is full, just try the next one.

To place an order, you must have a seat at a table. People standing in the walkways are not served.

Third, the buzz: What makes it worth visiting

The action happens in the beer halls. Most halls only serve a mass of beer, which is a glass that contains 1 liter of beer. The beer is stronger than normal, with an alcohol percentage content of about 6-7%, compared to the usual 4-5%. Put this potent beer together with the mixture of visitors coming from all over the world and you have a bizarre — but must see — gathering. Tables are shared by a mix of tourists, businesspeople, and locals. The majority are tipsy, and some are totally drunk, which creates an overall relaxed and funny atmosphere. Live music is played and people will start to dance on the benches and sing together with the musicians and people at neighboring tables.

If you are going with business partners or colleagues, I highly recommend that you reserve a table for your group. Going out together for an evening at Oktoberfest is a tremendous way to strengthen any relationship. It's an unforgettable experience and a must-do at least once in your lifetime.

The Empty-plate Challenge

A German friend or colleague may well invite you for a meal at their home. If you are from an Asian culture, you are likely taught from your childhood to leave something on the plate to show the host that they served you enough food and you are not hungry anymore. However, Germans usually finish everything on the plate, to show the host that they enjoyed the food and were served enough.

This may lead to an awkward situation when a German is a guest in an Asian home. The German guest finishes everything on their plate to show they liked the food, but then the Asian host refills the plate immediately, as they think that the guest is still hungry. After a couple of refills, the German guest usually gives up and refuses more food, most probably too late for the well-being of their stomach.

Finishing everything during a meal is a German custom; it doesn't mean that the guest is still hungry; a German host won't naturally refill your plate. As mentioned in other chapters, Germans expect you to speak up if you require something. Asking "May I have a bit more of your delicious Sauerkraut?" is no problem at all. Your host won't feel embarrassed, thinking that the portion offered was too small; the host will highly appreciate your request, as it shows that you like the food. A host also might ask, "Do you want more Sauerkraut?" Politely saying "no" won't offend. Just be open and clear on when you are full or want more.

There is only one thing that you should avoid: leaving too much on the plate. In this case, the host will ask if you didn't like the food. Replying "No, it's perfect" but leaving a significant amount will arouse suspicion. It's acceptable to leave a little food on the plate, to show it tasted good but you are full now.

YOU DON'T LIKE OUR FOOD?

Myself and three German colleagues had successfully finished a project with an Indian service provider, and we invited Ramesh, the Indian delivery manager, out for a dinner. We asked whether Italian cuisine was fine for him, and he agreed, so we went to a nice, well-known Italian restaurant in the city center of Nuremberg. We had enjoyed working with Ramesh, and so we planned an unforgettable evening for him. We explained the meal options to Ramesh and suggested a couple of dishes for him, as he was a vegetarian. Ramesh decided to go for pizza.

(*Continued*)

> Soon after we placed the order, our dishes arrived and we chowed down on everything. The food was delicious; however, Ramesh left more than half of his pizza on the plate. Of course, we asked whether he didn't like the food, but Ramesh denied this and said it tasted good. As you can imagine, none of us believed that he was telling the truth. This incident spoiled an otherwise pleasant evening. I'm sure that Ramesh's intention was to avoid embarrassing his hosts. But our perception was different, and the misunderstanding was detrimental to building trust for future teamwork.

Food

Of course, no book about Germany would be complete without discussing food. You can find German food all over the world in "authentic" German restaurants. But there's often times like going to a Chinese restaurant in Munich: You don't get just Chinese food, but usually a mixture of Chinese/Thai/Vietnamese/Indian cuisines. What you know as German cuisine might be a mixture of German/Austrian/Swiss/Hungarian food.

Authentic German food is heavy on meats, sauces, and salt. Typical dishes are:

- Schweinshaxn (pork knuckle)
- Bratwurst (grilled sausage)
- Knödel (different kind of dumplings)
- Kartoffel (potato in several varieties)
- Sauerkraut (cabbage)
- Weisswurst (Bavarian cooked sausage)
- Schnitzel (thin meat, breaded)
- Spätzle (soft noodles)
- Bretzel (salty bread, shaped into a twisted knot)
- All kinds of breads made from light and dark doughs

Additionally, there are these famous sweet treats:

- Stollen (bread-like cake with dried fruits, usually served during Christmas)
- Buchteln and Dampfnudel (sweet dumplings filled with jam, served in vanilla sauce)
- Krapfen (fried sweet dumplings filled with jam and glazed with white sugar)
- Topfenstrudel (layered pastry filled with soft cheese; dish of Austrian origin)
- Apfelstrudel (layered pastry filled with apple; dish of Austrian origin)
- Kaiserschmarrn (sweetish shredded pancake with thick apple sauce; dish of Austrian origin that's popular in South Germany)

The most popular non-German cuisine is Italian. Italian restaurants are everywhere, on every main roads of big cities, but also in small, rural villages. When dining with a bigger group, Italian food is a safe bet, as it offers something for everyone: noodles, pizza, salads, soups, seafood, and much more. It's also no problem for vegetarians and vegans to find something. Other popular cuisines are French, Greek, Turkish, and Middle Eastern. Restaurants aren't halal certified, so check with the owner whether the place is halal or not.

Asian food is widespread too; Chinese and Indian cuisines are the most popular, but Vietnamese, Thai, and Japanese cuisines are becoming more appealing. Note that the taste will be very different compared to the real deal. Most of the dishes are "Germanized," either by using local ingredients or reducing the spice level. Probably the most authentic Asian cuisine is Indian; it still tastes Germanized, but it is closer to the original than any other Asian cuisines.

Beverages

One word: beer. Germany has more than 1,300 breweries,[2] and most of them strictly follow the "Reinheitsgebot" (Beer Purity Law), which permits only water, hops, and malt as ingredients. Typical beers have an alcohol percentage content of around 5%. The most popular beer is lager, and in Germany, this is divided into Helles (with a malty character) and Pils (with a hoppy character), though the separation is hardly noticeable — for non-Germans, both are standard lagers. Weizen (wheat beer) is also very common, especially in Bavaria. The region around Cologne has Kölsch, a light-bodied pale lager. In recent years, craft-style beers such as ales and stouts have started to pop up in Germany, though it's still difficult to get them outside of specialty beer shops. Good luck trying to find an Indian pale ale on tap anywhere in Munich.

Nearly all restaurants and beer gardens also serve wine, often a lower-class wine that you can order it pure or with carbonated water ("Weinschorle"). High-quality wine is served in middle- to upper-class restaurants. Wines from Germany, Austria, France, and Italy are popular.

Other beverages are a pretty standard selection of cocktails and soft drinks. The coffee culture is very much focused on espresso rather than drip-brewed coffee.

Note that alcohol consumption is permitted in public places, like pavements, public squares, parks, and public transport. You can buy a bottle of beer in a supermarket, go outside, open it, and start to drink it immediately, even while walking — no need to cover the bottle. To non-Germans, it can be strange to see someone walking along with an opened half-liter bottle of beer in their hand and occasionally taking a sip from it.

---

[2] Deutscher Brauer-Bund e.V. Press release, March 2016, http://www.brauer-bund.de/

To Pay or Not to Pay?

Unlike other cultures, dining in a group in Germany often results in a shared bill. Either you divide the bill by the number of guests, or each individual adds up the cost of their dishes and then everybody pays exactly what their own meal costs.

If a German invites you out for a dinner — explicitly uses the word "invite" — then you can expect that person to pay for everything. "Invite" in this context in German doesn't mean just "inviting someone to join"; it explicitly means "inviting someone to join *and* the inviter will pay the bill."

Also, when the waiter brings the check, don't pretend that you want to pay. If you offer to pay, the offer will be gladly accepted. Don't expect a "fight" for the bill, like in many Asian cultures.

Driving "Culture"

Many stories are told about driving in Germany, especially about the famous Autobahn with no speed limit and cars that can go up to 280 kilometers per hour (175 miles per hour). Yes indeed, if the weather, road condition, visibility, and traffic allow, you can speed at 280 kilometers per hour or more. However, the reality is usually different. Officially, about 70%[3] of all Autobahn sections have no speed limit, but often, the traffic flows at about 120–140 kilometers per hour, and that makes it difficult to go faster. The Autobahn has two to four lanes for each direction, and the rule is that slower vehicles must drive in the right-hand lane and can only change lane to overtake (though drivers break that rule). Faster cars usually drive in the left-hand lanes. Nevertheless, you could be driving at 180 kilometers per hour in the left lane and find that a faster car is tailgating you and flashing its headlights to signal to you that you should change lane

---

[3] Federal Highway Research Institute: https://www.bast.de/BASt_2017/DE/Publikationen/Fachveroeffentlichungen/Verkehrstechnik/Downloads/V1-BAB-Tempolimit-2015.html

and give way. Tailgating is common on the Autobahn and results in multiple accidents each year.

The driving pace in cities is slower and quite orderly compared to other European or Asian cities. Take note that any collision between vehicles is taken very seriously, even the smallest contact resulting in no visible scratches or dents. Once damage occurs, often the police are called in. In case of a collision, stop your car as soon as possible and talk calmly with the other party involved. If you keep driving, you will most probably be charged with a hit-and-run, which will result in a court hearing. Once you stop, don't admit to, sign, or confirm anything, just wait until the police arrive. When they do, be corporative with them; the police will treat you fairly. Also, be aware of the traffic rules: If you run a red light or exceed the speed limit by 30 kilometers per hour, you will face a fine of at least 100 Euros and a suspension of your driving license for a couple of weeks.

Chapter 9

Final Words

The world is global. US technology organizations are everywhere, Asian companies are expanding their businesses into Europe, and Germans are building manufacturing facilities across Asia. In many industries, like information technology services and consumer goods manufacturing, Germany is a preferred customer. In other industries, like automotive and chemicals, Germany is a sought-after supplier. Economies are evolving radically, and a professional in any sector will eventually work with Germans.

What are the Advantages When Working with Germans?

- **Predictable duration and outcomes:** When you make an agreement, purchase a product, or execute a process, the duration and outcome usually match the agreed goal.
- **Timeliness:** Product deliveries, project milestones, or the start of a meeting — appointments and milestones are met.
- **Transparency:** If something doesn't run as planned, you will know about it. Making assumptions and reading between the lines aren't necessary, because problems are communicated openly and honestly.

- **No hidden agendas:** Meeting agendas are as written on paper. The surrounding context gets minor attention; the focus is on the agenda items, working through them one by one.
- **Top quality:** Goods produced in Germany are well known for their high-quality standard. Germans' adherence to rules and regulations, together with a well-designed process framework, makes them leaders in quality assurance.

What are the Disadvantages When Working with Germans?

- **Potential to cause offense:** Germans' direct way of saying what they think, being direct and to the point, and saying "no" right in your face can hurt people's feelings.
- **Potential to embarrass:** Issues are brought up directly and without considering the emotional context. Germans only state the facts at hand, but people who aren't used to this may feel blamed, which may affect someone's standing in an organization and cause embarrassment.
- **Lack of flexibility and spontaneity:** A process is predictable, which means it's difficult to cut corners, speed it up, or add other views or ways of working. A process runs as it is defined.
- **Fear of change:** Instead of welcoming changes, Germans see them as potential dangers and challenge them. Hence, it takes Germans a long time to accept and execute changes.
- **Negativity:** Complaining, moaning, blaming — Germans' focus on negativity may impact your mood. Cheer up, smile, and don't get infected by this negativity.

Germany has one of the most powerful economies in the world. It holds a key position in the European Union, and is at the forefront of several technological fields: automotive, chemicals, and research, for example. Germany is one of the largest exporters of goods in the world, and maintains a well-developed standard of living and social-security system.

So German behaviors can't be wrong, can they?

There is no such thing as a wrong or right behavior. There are simply cultures that are different: different in thinking, communication, and approaches. Dealing with a foreign culture, either in business life or private life, is challenging — and it can be inspiring, as you learn a new dimension of life. It's one of the most exciting adventures you can explore.

Observe and respect German behaviors.

Understand their way of communicating and you will understand your business partners.

As long you keep the basics of the foreign culture in mind, your encounters will be enjoyable experiences. The basics of the German culture can be summarized as:

Directness — Adherence — Commitment

- Directness:
  - Don't treat short and direct answers as offensive or disrespectful.
  - Express yourself directly, and don't expect Germans to read between the lines.
  - If something is unclear, ask immediately and directly for clarification.
  - Keep small talk to a minimum.
  - No feedback is good feedback.
  - Don't treat negative feedback as personal disapproval.
  - You don't lose face if you deny something or admit to failing.

- Adherence:
  - Bureaucracy, rules, and regulations are highly valued.
  - People are used to following rules and regulations, and so should you.
  - In most cases your status and personal connections will not

speed up a process.
- □ Germans are not risk takers, and don't expect flexibility or spontaneous decisions.
- □ Accept that Germans protect and defend their position.
- □ Don't be offended by the "know-it-all" behavior.

- Commitment:
  - □ Honor your commitments.
  - □ When you make a commitment, treat it seriously, no matter whether it's in business or private life.
  - □ If you foresee that you will not be able to deliver on a commitment, give your counterpart an early warning, before the commitment is due.
  - □ You won't lose face if you give an early warning, but you will damage your reputation if you ignore the commitment.
  - □ If you have no new information, communicate that you have no new information.
  - □ Keep the different communication styles of indirect and direct cultures in mind.
  - □ Once signed, contracts are binding.

Keep directness, adherence, and commitment in mind, and your experiences will be enjoyable.

If you find these points helpful, share them with others — your colleagues, friends, and family. Encourage everyone to share your enthusiasm, and inspire them to embark on exciting cultural journeys.

All in all, Germans are great to work and engage with.

Disclaimer:

This book talks about cultural standards. That means describing behaviors that most people have. Note: *most* people, not all people. In Germany there are people who are indirect and reserved, and people who don't care about rules and regulations. So please, always pay attention to an individual's character and be respectful of the person you're dealing with.

Appendix A

Frequently Asked Questions

Over the many years I've worked with international cultures, people have asked me questions and for tips on working with Germans. Below, I've summarized the most frequently asked questions and my personal responses.

I'm traveling to Austria and Switzerland. They also speak German there. Are they like Germans?

No, other German-speaking countries have different cultures. They do speak German, but in different regional dialects. The Austrian dialect is similar to the Bavarian dialect (South Germany), for example, but the Swiss dialect is quite different and can be difficult to understand, even for native German speakers. Also, from a cultural perspective the contrast can be huge. Austria, for example, has a similar set of rules to Germany. However, the compulsion to follow these rules is totally different. In Austria, people are flexible and adaptive and may find a way around rules. The culture is more relationship-oriented. When you travel across Austria, you'll notice the relaxed pace, and that people are friendly and open. Some points mentioned in this book don't apply in Austria and Switzerland, or at least, they do apply to a lesser extent.

Is there a cultural difference between East and West Germany?

Since 1990, Germany has been a united country consisting of the former West Germany (ten states) and East Germany (six states). Both countries had an opposing political system (democratic versus communistic), which led to tension after the merger, especially because the western states had to finance the economic development of the eastern states. But today, life is quite similar in all the states, despite the fact that the economy is still stronger in the western states and a lot of college graduates move from eastern to western states for work. When it comes to culture, foreigners won't notice any difference.

I often hear German colleagues use the phrase "as I already said..." when explaining something or replying to a question. It sounds like they think I'm an idiot and are blaming me for not listening to what they said. Why do they think I'm stupid?

When Germans speak English, they often translate German phrases word for word into English. In German, the phrase "*wie schon gesagt*" adds emphasis to the statement that follows the phrase. "As I already said" is just a literal translation of the German phrase, and it is not meant to have negative connotations. Nothing to worry about.

I received emails from Germans with sentences that end with multiple question or exclamation marks; for example, "can we do this???" And, "we decided on this already, last week!!!" This is bad manners. Why do they use this style?

Here, it's a matter of paying attention to the content of the sentence, not the perceived tone. Of course, the directness here doesn't help: "We decided on this already, last week" is a very direct statement that might offend. It's simply German directness, though. The additional punctuation marks are usually added by people who have no idea what that means in "internet etiquette." Pay attention to the content, but don't take the punctuation marks personally.

I've read stories about skinheads and Neo-Nazi, saying that they beat up foreigners. Is it safe in Germany for non-white people?

There were such occurrences in the past, and unfortunately, they still happen once in a while. But this aggression is usually concentrated in specific areas known for trouble, like the stadiums of specific soccer teams. In any business, urban, or tourist area, this is highly unlikely to happen. Germany has the strictest anti-racism law in the world and is a safe place. Apply common sense and avoid the trouble areas. How can you identify these areas? Just ask a colleague or the concierge of your hotel whether the area you plan to visit is safe.

Is Oktoberfest across Germany or just in a specific city?

This is the number-one question people ask me. Oktoberfest is just in a specific city, Munich. It's even in a specific place in Munich called Theresienwiese, a 1,000-by-500-meter area (120 acres). For more information, please see Chapter 8, "Oktoberfest."

How widely spoken is English? Will I face difficulties in work/shopping/dining?

It depends on the area you are visiting. Basic English is widely spoken in all the big cities. Staff in shops and restaurants do understand basic phrases for ordering. However, don't expect them to know the English words for German food. Other than in tourist centers, the waiting staff won't understand "pork knuckle"; you need to order "Schweinshaxe." English is also less common in eastern states, as traditionally their second language was Russian. However, language skills keep improving, and somehow you can get by with English nearly everywhere. In the business field, it's no problem at all: English is widely spoken.

I'm meeting a German business partner/ private host/relative for the first time. Should I bring a gift?

Gift-giving is not expected in German business conduct. But if you meet someone in private or are invited for a gathering at someone's house, a gift is appreciated. See Chapter 7, "Gifts."

Is tipping customary in Germany? And if so, how much should I tip?

Yes, tipping is customary in taxis, restaurants, bars, and anywhere else you sit down and are served at a table. The usual amount is 10–15%

when service was acceptable (there is hardly any *good* service). If the service was bad, don't tip. It's commonly accepted that you'll show that you're not satisfied and voice complaints; that's what locals do. You don't need to tip in retail stores, supermarkets, gas stations, or "over-the-counter shops" like bakeries, to-go coffee shops, and fast-food chains.

Are there really no speed limits on the highway?

Yes and no. It's true that there is no general speed limit on the Autobahn (highway). You can find more information in Chapter 8, "Driving culture". I used to arrive in Munich on a Sunday morning at 7 a.m., and it was just me and the Autobahn: A99, a 30-kilometer[1] distance, three lanes, and light traffic. That was an opportunity to go (way) faster than 130 kilometers per hour, which was an interesting experience.

How big a discount can I negotiate in shops?

In Germany, fixed prices are customary and price haggling is not expected or common. However, that doesn't mean you can't ask for a discount when shopping for electronics or clothes, especially if you're not interested in the latest stuff. Shopkeepers often reduce the price for such items, so just ask. Another option is to look at what the product costs online (for example, check on Amazon), and ask whether a local store will price-match. Use a price comparison website[2] to find out the best online price. Don't try haggling in restaurants and supermarkets, though.

---

[1] From Autobahnkreuz Muenchen Nord to Autobahnkreuz Muenchen Sued.
[2] A popular price-watch website for consumer electronics: http://www.geizhals.de.

How important is punctuality? Is it an issue to be 15 minutes late?

Appointments are precisely planned and punctuality is highly valued in Germany. It's impolite and definitively an issue to be 15 minutes late without notifying your host beforehand. Punctuality is seen as good manners, and if you don't take it seriously, your reputation will suffer. If you know that you will be late for a meeting, just inform your host as soon as possible. This is accepted and appreciated, and won't have a negative impact on your relationship.

How do I spell German time specifications?

Germany uses the 24-hour clock instead of the a.m./p.m. system. Many people understand a.m./p.m. but they never use it actively. Note that a time written as 17:30 or 1730 isn't "seventeen hundred thirty" but "seventeen thirty." To make matters more complicated, in spoken collegial language people prefer to say "We'll meet at five" to mean 17:00, but without adding a.m. or p.m. Sometimes they add "in the afternoon" or "in the morning," or say, "We'll meet at seven for dinner." Obviously, dinner implies that the time is 19:00. Apply common sense to understand which time is meant. If in doubt, it's not an issue to ask: "You mean eight o'clock on Saturday morning, right?"

I bought a U-Bahn ticket, but there are no turnstiles or access gates in U-Bahn stations. Can I just walk in? How do they know I bought a ticket?

Your ticket needs to be validated before you enter the station. Use a ticket validator — a small box with a ticket slot — to stamp your ticket. These ticket validators can be found close to the station entrance

(U-Bahn), or sometimes on the platforms (S-Bahn). Make sure you validate the ticket before boarding the train. Ticket inspectors conduct random checks. Once the ticket inspectors disclose their identity (showing a badge), they will check whether you bought the proper ticket and whether it's validated. If something is wrong, the passenger has to pay an "erhoehtes Befoerderungsentelt" (in English: a fine). Newer machines issue tickets that don't fit in the ticket validator. These are pre-validated and don't need to be stamped. If unsure, check with the platform operator before you travel.

Why are German words so long? What the heck is a "Rückversicherungsgesellschaft?"

The length of German nouns makes them look more complicated than they actually are. Germans connect words that are separate in other languages. A "Rückversicherungsgesellschaft" is a "re-insurance company." It consists of "Rück" (re-) + "Versicherung" (insurance) + "Gesellschaft" (company). The words "Versicherung" and "Gesellschaft" are nouns with the same meaning as insurance and company in English. Both nouns can be used separately in their own context. The difference is that when combining them in German, they are connected as a single word, and in English, they are separated by a space. Here's another example: time zone and Zeitzone. "Zeit" + "Zone" are separate nouns that have the same meaning as time and zone but are connected without a space.

Does Germany have a sales tax?

Yes, you pay 19% sales tax on all purchased goods (listed as Umsatzsteuer, Ust, or MwSt on a receipt). Some food and basic items have 7% sales tax. The tax rate is the same across all states. You can get a tax refund at the airport if you're not a citizen of a European Union country.

Is the healthcare system reliable? Do I have to pay for treatment on the spot?

The healthcare system and medical technology in Germany are among the best in the world. Doctors are highly educated, and hygiene standards are top-notch. The system consists of two types of healthcare insurance: the government insurance, for which a monthly fee is deducted from your salary, and the private insurance, for which you pay a lump sum. People with government insurance don't need to pay to visit a doctor; they present their insurance card and the clinic arranges the payment directly with the insurer. People with private insurance have to pay on the spot or via an invoice, and then they get the money back from their insurer. As a visitor, you have to pay on the spot and arrange the refund from your healthcare insurer. Healthcare costs are similar to those in other developed countries, but cheaper than in the United States.

Are credit cards accepted everywhere?

Not at all. Credit cards are accepted for public transport (long-distance trains and some suburban), and at gas stations, shops, and restaurants in big cities. But as soon you head off the beaten track, you find hardly any shops that accept credit-card payments. Cashless payment in Germany is done via debit cards issued by local banks (Bankkarte). To be on the safe side, always have some cash in your wallet.

Are all German dialects the same?

Beside a couple of different words for the same things, the written language is more or less the same in all German-speaking countries (Germany, Austria, Switzerland, and Lichtenstein). But each country speaks its own dialect. If you equate the language in Germany with

British English, then the language in Austria would be similar to American English. Different dialect, but both understand each other well. The Swiss dialect can be difficult to understand even for native speakers from Germany or Austria. The Lichtenstein dialect is a mix of (western) Austrian and Swiss.

Nobody honks in Germany, not even when overtaking. Isn't that dangerous?

I hear this question from my Indian colleagues quite often. Honking in Germany is definitely not part of driving etiquette. Overtaking, changing lines, and approaching a crossing don't call for honking. If somebody honks, it's not like the short "Here comes a car, take care" honk, it's more of a long "You idiot!" honk. Honking is perceived as aggressive, clearly showing that you think somebody else did something wrong. Don't honk unless it's absolutely necessary to avoid a crash.

Appendix B
Facts and Figures

Population: ~83 million
Area: ~357,000 square kilometers (~137,000 square miles)
Currency: Euro (1 Euro = 100 cents)
Capital: Berlin (population 3.6 million)
Time zone: CET (Central European Time) = UTC + 1, daylight saving from last Sunday in March until last Sunday in October

Federal states: 16
Baden-Württemberg, Bavaria, Berlin, Brandenburg, Bremen, Hamburg, Hesse, Mecklenburg-West Pomerania (Mecklenburg-Vorpommern), Lower Saxony, North Rhine-Westphalia, Rhineland-Palatinate (Rheinland-Pfalz), Saarland, Saxony, Saxony-Anhalt, Schleswig-Holstein, Thuringia
Form of government: Federal parliamentary democracy
Main religion: Christianity (about 65%)

Largest cities:

1. Berlin (3.6 million)
2. Hamburg (1.8 million)
3. Munich (1.4 million)

Highest mountain: Zugspitze, 2,962 meters (9,717 feet)
Universities: 370[1]

---

[1] https://www.deutschland.de/en

Cultural institutions:
6,200 museums, 820 theaters, 130 professional orchestras, 8,800 libraries

Climate:
Seasonal continental climate with cold winters and hot summers. The average daytime temperature in January is about 3°C (38°F) and in July it's 22°C (72°F). Extremes can reach −20°C (−4°F) in winter and 38°C (100°F) in summer.

Electricity:
220 volts/50 Hertz; EU plug (Schuko Stecker)

Country code:
+49 (phone), de (internet), GER (sports)

National flag:

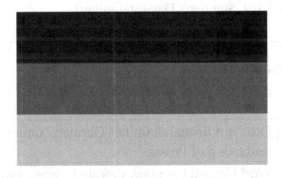

Nationwide public holidays:

Date	Holiday
January 1st	New Year's Day (Neujahr)
March/ April	Easter Monday (Ostermontag) (weekend following the first full moon after 21st March)
May 1st	Labor Day (Tag der Arbeit)
May	Ascension Day (Christi Himmelfahrt) (40 days after Easter)
June	Whit Monday (Pfingstmontag) (seventh Monday after Easter)
October 3rd	German Unity Day (Tag der deutschen Einheit)
December 25th	Christmas Day (Christtag)
December 26th	St. Stephen's Day (Stefanitag)

Historic milestones:

Year	Event
1871	Otto von Bismarck unifies Germany under the leadership of Prussia.
1914–18	World War I; Germany defeated, signs capitulation.
1919	Treaty of Versailles: Germany loses land to neighbors; beginning of the Weimar Republic.
1933	Hitler becomes chancellor. Weimar Republic gives way to a one-party state and Hitler proclaims the Third Reich in 1934.
1938	Annexation of Austria and Sudetenland.

(Continued)

1939–45	Invasion of Poland triggers World War II.
1945	Germany defeated, Hitler commits suicide. Allies divide Germany into four occupation zones (United States, United Kingdom, France, Soviet Union).
1949	Germany divided into two states: US, French, and British zones in the west become the Federal Republic of Germany; Soviet Union zone in the east becomes the communist German Democratic Republic. Konrad Adenauer of the Christian Democrats is West Germany's first chancellor.
1955	West Germany obtains independence and joins NATO; East Germany joins the Warsaw Pact.
1961	Construction of the Berlin Wall to end the escape of people from East to West.
1973	East and West Germany join the United Nations.
1987	East German leader Erich Honecker makes first official visit to West Germany.
1989	Mass movement of East Germans as neighboring countries reduce travel restrictions. Protests across East Germany lead to rapid collapse of communist rule and fall of the Berlin Wall.
1990	East Germany and West Germany unite and merge into the Federal Republic of Germany.
2002	Euro replaces Deutsche Mark.

Appendix C

Further Reading and Helpful Links

http://www.deutschland.de
Information portal about German language, education, jobs, economy, and more. Published in cooperation with the Federal Foreign Office in Berlin.

https://www.germany.travel
Website of the German National Tourist Board. Offers information about cities, culture, nature, castles, experiences, and everything else travel related.

http://www.auswaertiges-amt.de
Official webpage of the Federal Foreign Office Germany. Provides services regarding entry, residence, and Visa regulations.

http://www.bundesregierung.de
Official webpage of the Federal Government. A source of information material about demography, finance, and economics.

http://www.bundesgesundheitsministerium.de
Official webpage of the Federal Ministry of Health. A health guide about health care providers, diseases, vaccines, and drinking water.

http://www.goethe.de
The Goethe-Institute is the Federal Republic of Germany's cultural institute. They promote the study of German language and international cultural exchange.

http://www.spiegel.de
Popular news and journalism portal with an English section.

http://www.dw.com
Deutsche Welle, German broadcaster with an English media portal.

http://www.germanfoodguide.com
Quite detailed advice on German foods.

http://www.bahn.com
Information portal of Deutsche Bahn, the largest German railway company. The portal offers almost all tickets online and regular offers for fare discounts.

http://www.zoll.de
Official webpage of the German Customs Office. Provides information regarding import, export, taxes, and allowances for private individuals and companies.

http://dict.leo.org, http://www.woerterbuch.info
Popular German-English dictionaries.

http://www.rki.de
Webpage of the Robert Koch Institute. They are dedicated to the investigation and prevention of infectious diseases and are also responsible for nationwide health monitoring.

http://www.gtai.de
Economic development agency of Germany.

http://www.studying-in-germany.org
Information portal for international students who want to know more about studying and living in Germany.

http://www.ebay-kleinanzeigen.de
Largest portal for classifieds in Germany. You can find used cars, electronics, services, do-it-yourself stuff, and more.

http://www.stepstone.de, http://de.indeed.com, http://stellenmarkt.sueddeutsche.de
Popular search engines for finding jobs in Germany.

https://en.wikipedia.org/wiki/Culture_of_Germany
A quick read about aspects of German culture like language, literature, music, religion…

http://en.wikipedia.org/wiki/Chronemics
Covers the relationship between time and communication.

https://en.wikipedia.org/wiki/High-_and_low-context_cultures
Edward T. Hall's book *Beyond Culture* pioneers the subject of low- and high-context cultures.

http://www.db.com/research
Public research portal of Deutsche Bank covering economics, politics, and financial markets.

http://www.germany.info/
Information about Germany especially for United States citizens, e.g. visas, consulates, embassies, the economy, and more.

Appendix D

TL;DR[1]

Welcome to Germany, where rules and regulations are followed.

The Core Values of Germans are

Candor
Reliability
Commitment
A respect for facts and figures

When Dealing with Germans

Be direct

- Don't treat short and direct answers as offensive or disrespectful.
- Express yourself directly, and don't expect Germans to read between the lines.
- If something is unclear, ask immediately and directly for clarification.
- Keep small talk to a minimum.
- No feedback is good feedback.
- Don't treat negative feedback as personal disapproval.

---

[1] Internet slang for "too long; didn't read"; summarizes a long text (or a book in this case).

- You don't lose face if you refuse to do something or admit to failing.

Respect adherence

- Bureaucracy, rules, and regulations are highly valued.
- People are used to following rules and regulations, and so should you.
- Your status and personal connections will not speed up a process.
- Germans are not risk takers, and don't expect flexibility or spontaneous decisions.
- Accept that Germans protect and defend their position.
- Don't be offended by the "know-it-all" behavior.

Deliver on commitments

- Honor your commitments.
- When you make a commitment, treat it seriously, no matter whether it's in business or private life.
- If you foresee that you will not be able to deliver on a commitment, give your counterpart an early warning, before the commitment is due.
- You won't lose face if you give an early warning, but you will damage your reputation if you ignore the commitment.
- If you have no new information, communicate that you have no new information.
- Keep the different communication styles of indirect and direct cultures in mind.
- Once signed, contracts are binding.

Thanks for reading.

About the Author

Michael Staudacher has coached international teams in Germany to maximize the positive effects of cultural diversity. Before that, he gained more than 15 years of intercultural experience working for German multinational corporations across the globe. Michael explored cultures in Malaysia, India, China, and the United States, and analyzed how individuals communicate in complex organizations. His specialties are transformation, global standardization, and intercultural teams.

Before Michael embarked on his journey as an author, he was a manager at Intel Corporation. Michael holds no bachelor or master degree in information technology or any other field. In fact, he has never seen an university from the inside.

Michael loves snowboarding (even though he isn't a big fan of the winter season), riding twisty roads with a motorcycle, and he is an avid fan of electronic music.

Michael can be contacted under author.michaelstaudacher.com or linkedin.com/in/mstaudacher.

References

1. I use the term "counterpart" throughout to refer to the "Gegenüber," the person with whom you're interacting with, be it your spouse, a colleague, a business partner, your manager, or a foreigner you meet.
2. The four-sides model, Friedemann Schulz von Thun, German psychologist.
3. Hall, E.T. (1976). *Beyond Culture.*
4. Toor, A. (2016, September 27). Germany orders Facebook to stop collecting data on WhatsApp users. *The Verge.* Retrieved February 28, 2021, from http://www.theverge.com/2016/9/27/13071330/facebook-whatsapp-user-data-germany-privacy.
5. Essers, L. (2015, April 8). Google ordered by German authority to change privacy practices. *PC World.* Retrieved February 28, 2021, from http://www.pcworld.com/article/2907612/google-ordered-by-german-authority-to-change-privacy-practices.html.
6. Petroff, A., & Pagliery, J. (2015, November 11). Microsoft to store data in Germany to keep it from third parties. *CNN Business.* Retrieved February 28, 2021, from http://money.cnn.com/2015/11/11/technology/microsoft-germany-data-center-privacy.
7. More than 244,000 opt out of Google Street View in Germany. (2010, October 21). *Deutsche Welle: Made For Minds.* Retrieved February 28, 2021, from http://www.dw.com/en/more-than-244000-opt-out-of-google-street-view-in-germany/a-6133854
8. Young, S. (2016). *Micromessaging: Why Great Leadership is Beyond Words.* New York, America: McGraw-Hill Education.

9. Website of the Hofbraeuhaus in Munich, the original one: http://www.hofbraeuhaus.de.

10. "Mass" is a German word for a mug that holds 1 liter of beer. It's popular in southern Germany, especially in beer gardens and the Oktoberfest.

11. United States, U.S. Bureau of Labor Statistics. (n.d.). *Average Paid Holidays and Days of Vacation and Sick Leave for Full-Time Employees.* Retrieved February 28, 2021, from https://www.bls.gov/news.release/ebs.t05.htm

12. Works Constitution Act (Betriebsverfassungsgesetz, BetrVG). (n.d.). Retrieved February 28, 2021, https://www.gesetze-im-internet.de/englisch_betrvg/index.html

13. Hanser, Kira. (2016, May 13). Weshalb Deutsche bei Kellnern gefürchtet sind. *Welt Online.* Retrieved February 28, 2021, from https://www.welt.de/reise/article155313788/Weshalb-Deutsche-bei-Kellnern-gefuerchtet-sind.html

14. Deutscher Brauer-Bund e.V. Press release, March 2016, http://www.brauer-bund.de/

15. Anker, Stefan. (2013, November, 3). Freie Fahrt — Wo geht das noch in Deutschland? *Welt Online.* Retrieved February 28, 2021, from https://www.welt.de/motor/article121455433/Freie-Fahrt-Wo-geht-das-noch-in-Deutschland.html

16. From Autobahnkreuz Muenchen Nord to Autobahnkreuz Muenchen Sued.

17. A popular price-watch website for consumer electronics: http://www.geizhals.de.

18. Your link to Germany. (n.d.). Retrieved February 28, 2021, from https://www.deutschland.de/en

19. Internet slang for "too long; didn't read"; summarizes a long text (or a book in this case).

Index